THE USBORNE
INTERNET-LINKED
LIBRARY OF SCIENCE
WORLD OF
PLANTS

Laura Howell, Kirsteen Rogers
and Corinne Henderson

Designed by Karen Tomlins, Chloë Rafferty,
Candice Whatmore and Adam Constantine

Digital illustrations by Verinder Bhachu
Digital imagery by Joanne Kirkby

Edited by Laura Howell

Cover design: Nicola Butler

Consultants: Dr Margaret Rostron and Dr John Rostron

Web site adviser: Lisa Watts
Editorial assistant: Valerie Modd

Managing designer: Ruth Russell
Managing editor: Judy Tatchell

INTERNET LINKS

If you have access to the Internet, you can visit the Web sites we have recommended in this book. On every page, you will find descriptions of what is on each Web site, and why they are worth visiting. Here are some of the things you can do on the recommended sites in this book:

- see amazing images of various plant parts under a powerful electron microscope

- play interactive quizzes, puzzles and games about many aspects of plant science

- visit online museums of different plant species

- watch animated movies about plant science topics such as photosynthesis and pollination

- find out about the weird and wonderful world of fungi, using games, pictures and activities

USBORNE QUICKLINKS

To visit the recommended sites in this book, go to the Usborne Quicklinks Web site, where you'll find links you can click on to take you straight to the sites. Just go to *www.usborne-quicklinks.com* and follow the simple instructions you find there.

Sometimes, Web addresses change or sites close down. We regularly review the sites listed in Quicklinks and update the links if necessary. We will provide suitable alternatives at *www.usborne-quicklinks.com* whenever possible. Occasionally, you may get a message saying that a site is unavailable. This may be a temporary problem, so try again later.

DOWNLOADABLE PICTURES

Pictures marked with the symbol ★ may be downloaded for your own personal use, for example, for homework or for a project, but may not be used for any commercial or profit-related purpose. To find these pictures, go to Usborne Quicklinks and follow the instructions there.

USING THE INTERNET

You can access most of the Web sites described in this book with a standard home computer and a Web browser (this is the software that enables you to access Web sites and view them on your computer).

Some Web sites need extra programs, called plug-ins, to play sounds or to show videos or animations. If you go to a site and you don't have the right plug-in, a message saying so will come up on the screen. There is usually a button you can click on to download the plug-in. Alternatively, go to Usborne Quicklinks and click on Net Help, where you will find links to plug-ins.

INTERNET SAFETY

Here are three important guidelines to follow to keep you safe while you are using the Internet:

- If a Web site asks you to register or log in, ask permission from your parent or guardian before typing in any information.

- Never give out personal information, such as your home address or phone number.

- Never arrange to meet someone that you communicated with on the Internet.

www.usborne-quicklinks.com

Go to Usborne Quicklinks for:

- direct links to all the Web sites described in this book

- free downloadable pictures, which appear throughout this book marked with a ★ symbol

SEE FOR YOURSELF

The *See for yourself* boxes in this book contain experiments, activities or observations which we have tested. Some recommended Web sites also contain experiments, but we have not tested all of these. This book will be used by readers of different ages and abilities, so it is important that you do not tackle an experiment on your own, either from the book or the Web, that involves equipment that you do not normally use, such as a kitchen knife or cooker. Instead, ask an adult to help you.

CONTENTS

7   Plants and fungi

8   Plant cells

10 Stems and roots

12 Plant tissue

14 Inside older plants

16 Leaves

18 Leaf structure

20 Movement of fluids

22 Plant food

26 Plant sensitivity

28 Flowering plants

32 Seeds and fruit

36 New plants from old

38 Water plants

40 Flowerless plants

42 Fungi

44 Fighting for survival

46 Plant lifestyles

48 Plants and people

50 Natural cycles

52 Classifying plants

54 Genetics

56 Useful plants and fungi

57 Test yourself

58 A-Z of scientific terms

62 Index

64 Acknowledgements

PLANTS AND FUNGI

Plants are the only living things that can make food in their own cells, using energy from the Sun. Fungi are plant-like, but lack the green chemical needed to make food; instead, they feed on living or dead matter. Like other living things, plants and fungi can grow, reproduce and react to the world around them. This book investigates the fascinating lives of plants and fungi, and the vital roles they both play on Earth.

The chemical that gives plants their green colour is what enables them to make their own food. Green plants, such as this cabbage, absorb sunlight through their leaves, and use it to make simple sugars.

PLANT CELLS

Every living thing is made up of tiny structures called **cells**. A plant has a number of different types of cells, and each one plays an important part in keeping it alive, such as absorbing water and minerals or making food.

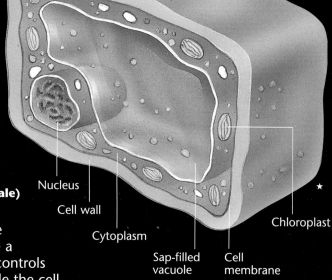

Typical plant cell (cutaway – not to scale)

Nucleus

Cell wall

Cytoplasm

Sap-filled vacuole

Cell membrane

Chloroplast

★

CELL STRUCTURE

Plant cells have many features in common with animal cells, but are generally larger. Plant cells also have a number of unique structures, most of which help the plant to make its own food.

Around each plant cell is a **cell wall**. This is made of a tough substance called **cellulose**, and helps the cell to keep its shape. Directly beneath the cell wall is a thin layer called the **cell membrane**. Animal cells also have a cell membrane, but they do not have a cell wall.

Vacuoles are fluid-filled sacs. Most plant cells have one large, permanent vacuole filled with a sugary liquid called **cell sap**, which is made up of water and dissolved substances.

All plant cells, like animal cells, have a **nucleus**, which controls the activities inside the cell. The nucleus is surrounded by a gel-like fluid called **cytoplasm**, within which smaller structures, called **organelles**, are moved and arranged. These have different functions.

Chloroplasts, for example, are organelles which contain a green chemical called **chlorophyll**. These give plants their colour and help to make food.

Chloroplast

Chromoplasts have a similar function. They give some flowers, and vegetables such as carrots, their particular colour.

See for yourself

You can use a microscope to look at plant cells. First, you need a slice of raw onion. Take one segment from the slice, and use tweezers to remove the thin membrane that covers it. Place the membrane on a glass microscope slide and look at it through a microscope, lighting it from beneath. You may be able to see the nucleus and the cell walls.

Cell wall

Nucleus

This is what leaf cells look like under a microscope. The dark spots inside the cells are the nuclei.

SPECIALIZED CELLS

Not all plant cells are exactly alike. Some have different shapes and structures, allowing them to do particular jobs. This is called **specialization**.

Palisade cells, for example, are found just beneath the upper surface of a leaf. They are column shaped, and contain a large number of chloroplasts.

Palisade cells

Spongy cells are found inside a leaf, beneath the layer of palisade cells. They have an irregular shape, which allows air spaces to form between them.

Spongy cells

Air space

CELL DIVISION

Cells can divide to create new cells for growth or repair. Cell division happens in two stages. In the first stage, called **mitosis**, the nucleus divides into two parts, each becoming a new nucleus. Each of the two new nuclei, called **daughter nuclei**, are identical to the original.

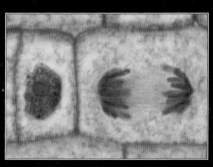

This microscope image shows the contents of a nucleus dividing in two.

In the second stage of cell division, called **cytokinesis**, a dividing line called the **cell plate** forms. This runs down the middle of the cytoplasm. New cell walls build up along the cell plate, to separate the two new cells.

Cytokinesis in a plant cell

Plant cell after mitosis has taken place

Cell plate forming

New cell wall forming

PLANT TISSUE

Cells of the same kind join together to form types of **tissue**. Most plants are made up of three types of tissue: dermal, ground and vascular.

Dermal tissue makes up the surface layer of most plants.

Dermal tissue

Ground tissue packs out most of the inside of younger plants.

Ground tissue

Vascular tissue is responsible for transporting food, water and other substances around the plant. For more about this, see page 12.

Vascular tissue

For more about this, see page 12.

STEMS AND ROOTS

A plant is mainly supported by its stem and roots. In most plants, these also play an important part in carrying fluids. The stem and roots are made up of various parts, which change as the plant gets older. You can find out more about these changes on pages 14-15.

STEM STRUCTURE

The **stem** is the major above-ground or **aerial** part of a plant. It supports the plant, usually growing upwards. Stems contain a system of **vascular tissue**, which carries water and minerals throughout the plant.

A **shoot** is a new stem which grows out of a seed or off the main stem of a plant. A **bud** is a small growth on a stem, which develops into either a new shoot or a flower. There are two different kinds of buds, called **terminal** and **axillary buds**. Axillary buds are also known as **lateral** or **secondary buds**.

A **terminal bud** is a bud growing at the end of a stem or shoot.

A **node** is the place on a stem where a leaf has grown.

An **internode** is the area of a stem or shoot between two nodes.

An **axillary bud** is found between a shoot or leaf stalk and the stem. This spot is called an **axil**.

Main parts of a stem

This thick stem contains a system of tubes, which carry water and food through the plant.

GROWTH

A group of cells which divide to provide new growth is called a **meristem**. The main meristems are at the tip of the shoot and root. They are called **apical meristems**. A meristem formed in the main stem or a shoot is part of a terminal bud.

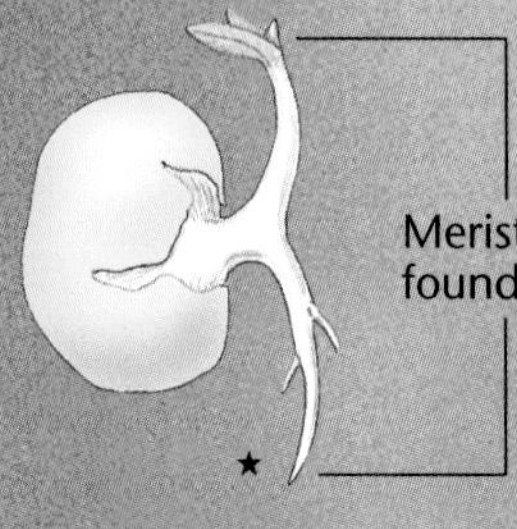

Meristems are found here.

★

10

PARTS OF A ROOT

The **root** of a plant usually grows down into the ground. Its main purpose is to take in water and minerals from the soil. These are absorbed through tiny, tube-shaped cells called **root hairs**. The root also acts as an anchor, holding the plant firmly in the soil.

A root grows when cells just behind its tip divide. This area is called the **growing point**. The area of new cells produced is called the **zone of elongation**. The new cells have soft cell walls, which allow them to stretch lengthways as water is taken into the root.

As the new cells lengthen, they push the tip of the root further into the soil. A layer of cells called the **root cap** protects the root tip as it is pushed down into the ground.

Parts of a root

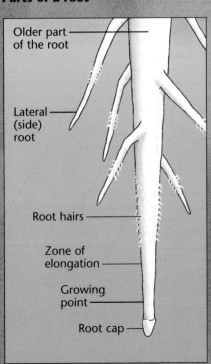

Older part of the root

Lateral (side) root

Root hairs

Zone of elongation

Growing point

Root cap

★

• Bulbs, 36

TYPES OF ROOTS

Roots can be many shapes and sizes, depending on the plant from which they grow. Some have particular tasks, such as allowing the plant to cling to other objects.

A **tap root**, or **primary root**, is a large root with smaller ones growing out of it. These small roots are called **lateral roots** or **secondary roots**. Many vegetables, such as carrots, are swollen tap roots and are known as **root vegetables**.

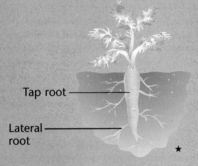

Tap root

Lateral root

★

Fibrous roots are a system of many equal-sized roots, all of which produce smaller lateral roots.

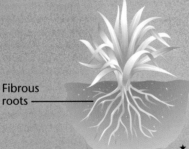

Fibrous roots

★

Adventitious roots grow directly from a stem. They are produced from gardeners' cuttings, or grow out of a special kind of stem called a bulb*.

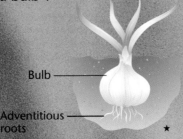

Bulb

Adventitious roots

★

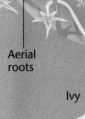

Aerial roots do not normally grow in the ground. Many can absorb moisture from the air. Some plants, such as ivy, also use them for climbing.

Aerial roots

Ivy

Prop roots are a particular kind of aerial root that grow outwards from a stem, then down into the ground. They support heavy plants, such as mangroves, which grow in ground which is often under water.

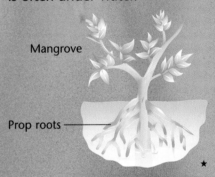

Mangrove

Prop roots

★

See for yourself

Look at a plant, and see how many parts of its stem you can identify. Notice what shapes and sizes they are. Be careful not to damage the plant.

Internet links

• Go to **www.usborne-quicklinks.com** for a link to the **Microscopy UK Web site** where you can read an easy-to-understand description of cell division and see lots of images of root cell division.

• Go to **www.usborne-quicklinks.com** for links to the **Wayne's Word Web site** to find detailed information about stems and roots, with clear photos and diagrams, as well as links to related topics. On this Web site you can also find out how strong plant roots can be.

• Go to **www.usborne-quicklinks.com** for a link to the **Ohio State University Web site** where you can take a thorough look at different types of roots and stems, with useful diagrams and photographs.

PLANT TISSUE

All plants, except for algae, mosses and liverworts, are known as **vascular plants**. This means that they contain a complex system of **vascular tissue**, which gives support and carries food and water through the plant.

TISSUE TYPES

Vascular tissue is made up of two main kinds of tissue, called xylem and phloem.

Water is carried up from the roots by **xylem**. In flowering plants, this is made up of short tubes called **vessels** and long, narrow tubes called **tracheids**. Long, thin cells called **fibres** help to provide support between them. Vessels are made up of column-shaped cells that have lost their dividing walls. Non-flowering plants have only tracheids.

Food made in the leaves dissolves in water and is carried to all parts of the plant by **phloem**. This is made up of fluid-carrying cells called **sieve tubes**. These have other cells packed around them for support.

Sieve tubes are arranged in long columns. They have cell walls*, and though they do not have a nucleus*, they are living cells with a thin layer of cytoplasm*. The end walls between the cells, called **sieve plates**, have tiny holes which allow liquids to pass through.

The first tissue formed by a new plant is called **primary tissue**. The xylem is **primary xylem** and the phloem is **primary phloem**.

There is vascular tissue inside these tulip stems. It supports the plant and takes food and water around it.

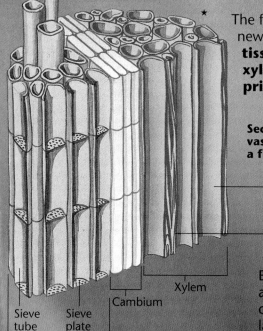

Section of vascular tissue in a flowering plant

Vessel

Fibre

Xylem

Cambium

Sieve tube

Sieve plate

Phloem

Between the xylem and phloem is a layer of thin, narrow-walled cells called **cambium**. The cells in this layer are able to divide, making more xylem and phloem.

Cell wall, Cytoplasm, Nucleus, 8.

INSIDE A STEM

In young stems, vascular tissue is usually arranged in groups called **vascular bundles**. These are surrounded by tissue called cortex. In plants known as dicotyledons*, the bundles are arranged in a regular pattern, as shown below.

Cross section of a young dicotyledon stem

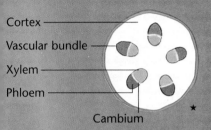

Cortex
Vascular bundle
Xylem
Phloem
Cambium
★

Cutaway of a young dicotyledon stem

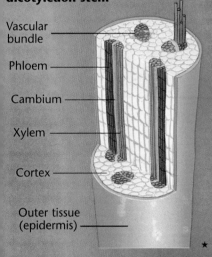

Vascular bundle
Phloem
Cambium
Xylem
Cortex
Outer tissue (epidermis)
★

In older dicotyledon stems, the bundles join up to form a central core called the **vascular cylinder**. You can read more about vascular tissue in older plants on page 14.

In plants known as monocotyledons*, such as the tulip on the left, the vascular bundles are not arranged regularly in the stem.

INSIDE A ROOT

In a young root, the tissue is arranged in a different way from a stem. A central core forms as the plant gets older.

Cross section of a young dicotyledon root

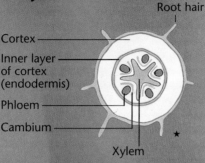

Root hair
Cortex
Inner layer of cortex (endodermis)
Phloem
Cambium
Xylem
★

Cutaway of a young dicotyledon root

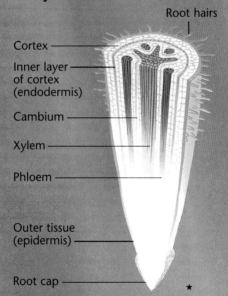

Root hairs
Cortex
Inner layer of cortex (endodermis)
Cambium
Xylem
Phloem
Outer tissue (epidermis)
Root cap
★

See for yourself

Try this experiment to see the xylem in a stick of celery. Fill a jar with about three centimetres of water, and add a few drops of ink or food colouring. Trim the end off a fresh celery stalk and stand it in the water. After a couple of hours, you can see the xylem as a pattern of coloured dots in the end of the stalk.

Xylem (seen as dots)

OTHER TISSUES

All parts of a young plant are surrounded by a thin layer of tissue called the **epidermis**. In older stems, the epidermis is replaced by bark. In older roots, it is replaced by a layer of hardened cells called the **exodermis**, then by bark. An outer tissue which encloses a plant, such as the epidermis, is known as **dermal tissue**.

The epidermis of stems and roots surrounds an area of **cortex**. In roots, this has an area called **endodermis** as its innermost layer. Cortex is made up mainly of **parenchyma**, a type of tissue with large cells and many air spaces. In some plants there is also some **collenchyma**, a type of supporting tissue with long, thick-walled cells. These are both types of ground tissue*.

The top layer of the epidermis is known as the **cuticle**. It is made of a waxy substance called **cutin**. The cuticle prevents a plant from losing or absorbing too much water.

Waxy cuticle gives these leaves their shiny appearance.

Internet links

• Go to **www.usborne-quicklinks.com** for links to the **Online Biology Book Web site** where you can find a thorough overview of plant structure, with lots of useful photographs and diagrams.

• Go to **www.usborne-quicklinks.com** for a link to the **Microscopy UK Web site** to find a detailed look at tissue in a non-woody plant. The Web page also has microscope images of cells in turgid and wilting plants (see page 21).

• Go to **www.usborne-quicklinks.com** for a link to **The Wonderful World of Biology Web site** to read a lengthy but logical look at plant structure.

* Dicotyledons, 53; Ground tissue, 9; Monocotyledons, 53.

INSIDE OLDER PLANTS

Plants which live for many years, such as trees, form new tissue to support their original primary tissue. This process is known as **secondary thickening**. The new tissue is made up of more fluid-carrying tissue, formed towards the middle of the plant, and protective tissue, formed on the outside.

TISSUE GROWTH

The production of new tissue in young stems, called **secondary tissue**, happens in stages. The process is slightly different in roots, but the overall result is the same.

In a stem, secondary thickening starts when more cambium (growth tissue) forms between the vascular bundles*. This joins up to form a continuous cylinder of tissue.

The cambium starts to produce more xylem and phloem. These join up to form a **vascular cylinder**. Each year, new layers of xylem and phloem are produced.

Over time, the stem and roots thicken, and the plant becomes known as a **woody plant**. The new xylem is **secondary xylem**, and the new phloem is **secondary phloem**.

The core of vascular tissue, which is mostly xylem, gets bigger. By this stage, the xylem is also called **wood**. The phloem does not widen as much because the xylem pushes it outwards.

Young stem
- Vascular bundle
- Xylem
- Cambium
- Phloem

Slightly older
- Xylem
- Cambium joins up.
- Phloem

Older still
- Xylem
- Cambium
- Phloem
- Xylem and phloem join up to form vascular cylinder.

After another year
- First layer of secondary xylem
- Cambium
- First layer of secondary phloem

After a number of years

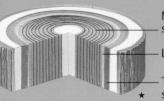

- Many layers of secondary xylem
- Layer of cambium
- ★ Thinner layers of secondary phloem

Giant sequoia trees may live for over 2,500 years. They develop lots of secondary tissue.

Vascular bundles, 13.

TYPES OF WOOD

A single ring of xylem in a cross section of an older plant shows one year's growth and is called an **annual ring**. Each ring has two separate areas – **spring wood** and **summer wood**.

Soft spring wood (also called **early wood**) forms rapidly early in the growing season. It has large cells. Harder summer wood, or **late wood**, is produced later on. Its cells are smaller and more closely packed together.

Annual rings in a tree stump

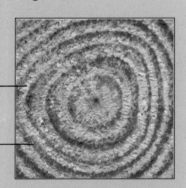

Light spring wood, with widely spaced cells, develops first.

Darker summer wood, with densely packed cells, develops later.

After a number of years, the annual rings themselves can also be divided into two separate areas. The area nearest the middle, where the rings are older, is called **heartwood**. Its vessels* have become solid and can no longer transport fluids, but they still provide the plant with support.

The outer area of rings is called **sapwood**. Its vessels are still able to carry fluid. Sapwood also helps to support the tree.

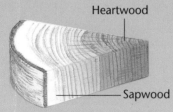

Heartwood

Sapwood

See for yourself

You can count the rings in a tree stump to discover the tree's age. For example, fifty rings show that the tree was fifty years old when it was cut down.

OUTER TISSUE

As well as new vascular tissue, an older plant also forms extra layers of protective tissue around its outside. These develop from a single layer of constantly dividing cells called **phellogen** or **cork cambium**.

As each new outer layer formed by the phellogen is pushed further out by new layers on its inside, it dies away to become waterproof **bark**. This contains tiny raised openings called **lenticels**, through which oxygen and carbon dioxide are exchanged. As a tree gets older, the layers of bark build up, making the trunk thicker and stronger.

Structure of bark in a mature tree

Outer bark

Inner bark

A lenticel. Loosely packed cells allow gases to move.

Bark stops the tree from drying out and helps to protect it from disease. It cannot grow or stretch, so it splits or peels as the trunk gets wider, and new layers of bark develop underneath.

Some types of bark

Silver birches have tough, papery bark.

English oak bark develops deep cracks.

Scots pine bark flakes off in small pieces.

Beech trees have very thin bark.

Internet links

• Go to **www.usborne-quicklinks.com** for a link to the **Dragonfly Web site** where you can learn more about trees. You can also design your own tree, and find out how it would cope in different climates.

• Go to **www.usborne-quicklinks.com** for a link to the **Domtar Web site** where you can find lots of fascinating information about trees, as well as a variety of games and experiments.

• Go to **www.usborne-quicklinks.com** for a link to the **Wayne's Word Web site** to have a look at annual rings and how they form.

• Go to **www.usborne-quicklinks.com** for a link to the **Bark, Wood, Roots and Leaves Web pages** where you can see a well-illustrated look at bark, wood, roots and leaves.

*Vessels, 12.

LEAVES

The **leaves** of a green plant are its main food-making parts. They make food by a process called **photosynthesis**. A plant's leaves are collectively called its **foliage**. There are many different sizes and shapes of leaves, but only two main types: simple and compound leaves.

SIMPLE LEAVES

Simple leaves are made up of a single leaf blade, called a **lamina**. Lilies, elms and maples are examples of plants with simple leaves.

Maple leaf

COMPOUND LEAVES

Compound leaves are made up of small leaf blades called **leaflets**, which grow from a central leaf stalk. Clovers and ferns are examples of plants with compound leaves. The number and arrangement of leaflets on a compound leaf vary from plant to plant.

Palmate leaves have five or more leaflets growing from a single point.

Horse chestnut

Trifoliate leaves have three leaflets growing from a single point.

White clover

Ternate leaves are a type of trifoliate leaf. Each leaflet is made up of three lobes.

Columbine

In **pinnate leaves** the leaflets, called **pinnae**, are arranged in opposite pairs along the stalk.

— Pinna

Pinnate leaf

A **bipinnate** or **tripinnate leaf** is a pinnate leaf with pinnate leaflets.

Bipinnate leaf

Tripinnate leaf

This fern's pinnate leaves have pinnate leaflets.

LEAF ARRANGEMENTS

Leaves can be arranged on a stem in several ways. **Opposite leaves**, for example, are leaf pairs whose members grow from opposite sides of the stem. **Decussate leaves** are opposite leaves in which each pair is at right angles to the one before.

This box has opposite leaves.

This purple loosestrife has decussate leaves.

Perfoliate leaves are single or paired leaves. The bases of the leaves surround the stem.

The leaves of this yellow-wort are perfoliate.

A **rosette** or **whorl** describes a circle of leaves which grow from one point. An example of this is a **basal rosette**, which grows at the base of a stem.

A primrose has leaves which form a basal rosette.

Alternate leaves grow individually from the stem, rather than in groups or pairs. **Spiral leaves** are alternate leaves which grow out from separate points that form a spiral around the stem.

This orpine has spiral leaves.

SPECIALIZED LEAVES

Some leaves are adapted to do particular jobs. They are usually found on plants that grow in a particular place or climate.

A **bract** is a leaf at the base of a flower stalk. It often protects buds.

— Bract

A pair of **stipules** grow at the base of a leaf stalk. They protect a bud as it forms.

Stipules

A **tendril** is a special thread-like leaf or stem, which either twines around or sticks to a support.

Tendril —

A **spine** is a modified leaf, which is thin and sharp. It has a much smaller surface area than most leaves, which prevents it from losing too much water.

This barrel cactus has many thin spines.

LEAF MARGINS

The edge of a leaf is known as the **leaf margin**. Some margins have a special shape, to help the plant's survival. For example, a leaf with a wavy margin allows more light to reach the leaves beneath. Some common leaf margins are described below.

An **entire** leaf margin has no indentation of any kind.

Lilac

A **serrate** leaf margin has tiny jagged teeth.

Lime

A **lobed** leaf margin forms sections, called **lobes**. It may also be serrate.

English oak

See for yourself

Collect some fresh leaves that have recently fallen from trees or other plants, and compare their shapes and arrangements. To preserve leaves, you can flatten them between sheets of tissue or blotting paper under some heavy books. Leave them for two weeks to dry out.

Internet links

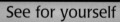

• Go to **www.usborne-quicklinks.com** for a link to the **Evergreen Project Web site** where you can read a good summary of all kinds of simple and compound leaves.

• Go to **www.usborne-quicklinks.com** for a link to the **Microscopy UK Web site** where you can find out what varnish "casts" of leaf surfaces look like viewed under a microscope.

LEAF STRUCTURE

L eaves are specially adapted to allow food production to take place. For example, most leaves have a broad, flat surface to collect sunlight, which is vital for making food. They also have areas which let out the waste substances created in the process.

INSIDE A LEAF

A leaf contains long strips of vascular tissue* called **veins**. These supply the leaf with water and minerals, and move the food made inside the leaf to other parts of the plant.

Some leaves, such as grasses, have long, parallel veins, but most contain one central vein called the **midrib**. This is an extension of the leaf stalk. The midrib branches into a number of smaller veins, called **side veins**. A leaf's whole vein system is called its **venation**.

Arrangement of leaf veins

Side vein

Midrib

LEAF CELLS

A leaf is made up of layers of different types of cells. The **epidermis** is a layer of flat, waxy cells on the surface of the leaf. It prevents too much water from being gained or lost.

The **palisade layer** lies just beneath the epidermis, on the leaf's upper side. It is made up of column-shaped **palisade cells**, which contain many tiny green chloroplasts*. The contents of palisade cells are packed closely together, which helps them to absorb sunlight (see page 22).

Under the palisade layer is the **spongy layer**, made up of irregularly shaped **spongy cells** and air spaces. The spaces allow air to move around inside the leaf. The spongy layer and palisade layer together are called the **mesophyll**.

Cross section of a leaf

Upper epidermis

Lower epidermis

Spongy cells

Palisade cells

Vascular tissue

Air space

Veins

*

SURFACE OF A LEAF

On the underside of a leaf are tiny holes called **stomata**, each one called a **stoma**. These allow water and air to move in and out of the leaf.

On either side of each stoma is a crescent-shaped **guard cell**. These paired cells can change their shape to open and close the stoma, controlling how much air and water enters and leaves the leaf.

Close-up of stoma (cut in half)

Stoma (open)

Guard cell

Stoma (closed)

* Chloroplasts, 8, 22; Vascular tissue, 12.

LEAF STALKS

A **leaf stalk** or **petiole** is a thin structure which joins the main body of a leaf to the stem. It contains the **leaf trace**. This is an area of vascular tissue which branches off the vascular tissue of a stem and becomes the leaf's central vein. This vein allows minerals to be carried into the leaf.

Leaf stalk
(petiole)

Before a leaf dies, a layer of cells called an **abscission layer** forms at the base of its stalk. The abscission layer separates the leaf from the rest of the plant. The leaf then falls off, creating a **leaf scar** on the stem.

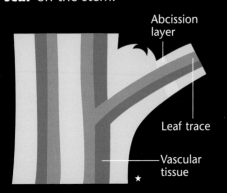

Abcission layer

Leaf trace

Vascular tissue

★

When leaves are dying, their green chlorophyll breaks down to reveal other colours.

COLOUR IN LEAVES

Leaves get their colour from chemicals called **pigments**. Most leaves are green because they contain a green pigment called chlorophyll. **Variegated leaves** are patterned because they only have pigments in certain places on their surface.

Other pigments include **xanthophylls**, which produce yellow shades, and **carotene**, which makes leaves look red or orange. These pigments are present in many plants, but are usually masked by chlorophyll. After summer has ended, the chlorophyll in most plants breaks down, revealing the other pigments.

See for yourself

Collect leaves that have fallen from different trees and compare their colours. See if you can find a plant with variegated leaves, or one whose leaves are a colour other than green all year round. These contain pigments in addition to green chlorophyll.

Internet links

• Go to **www.usborne-quicklinks.com** for a link to the **Science Made Simple Web site** to find an easy-to-read summary of how and why leaves change colour.

• Go to **www.usborne-quicklinks.com** for a link to the **Clemson University Web site** where you can find a detailed look at autumn leaf colours.

• Go to **www.usborne-quicklinks.com** for a link to the **Chemical of the Week Web pages** to learn about the chemistry behind leaf colour change.

• Go to **www.usborne-quicklinks.com** for a link to the **Microscopy UK Web site** to find out how leaf tissue arrangement varies in different conditions.

MOVEMENT OF FLUIDS

Fluids, such as water, need to reach all the parts of a plant for its cells to stay healthy. A plant's fluids are carried by its **vascular tissue**, made up of xylem and phloem. The **xylem** carries water from the roots to the leaves, and the **phloem** carries dissolved foods from the leaves to all other areas. The movement of fluids inside a plant is called **translocation**.

WATER MOVEMENT

Water is taken into a plant by its roots, and travels up in the xylem, through the stem to the leaves. There, some of it escapes as vapour through tiny holes called **stomata** on the underside of the leaves. This type of water loss is called **transpiration**.

As the outer leaf cells lose water by transpiration, the concentration of minerals and sugars inside them increases. So water from the cells further in passes into the outer cells, to replace the water that has been lost.

The inner cells in turn take water from cells further down, and so on. Water is "pulled" up through the plant from the roots, which take in more from the soil. This upward movement of water is called a **transpiration stream**.

At certain times, such as at night or on a damp, humid day, the rate of transpiration slows down. However, water from the soil continues to enter the roots. This is because it still has a weak attraction to the xylem walls, which drags it upwards. This is called **capillary action**.

As water is taken into the roots, **root pressure** begins to build up. This is strong enough to push the water up the stem and into the stream.

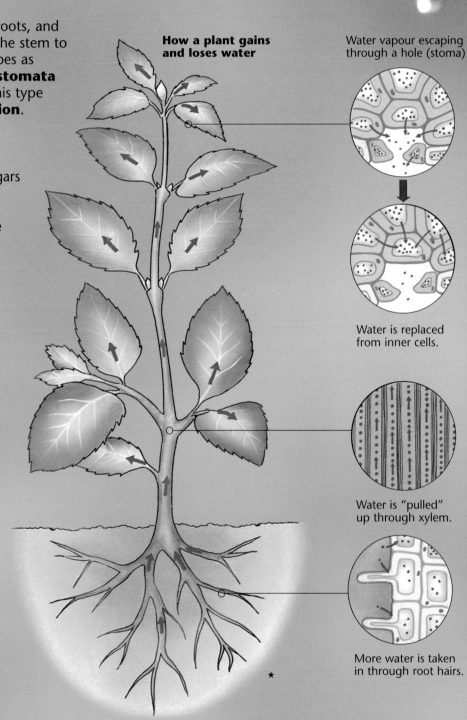

How a plant gains and loses water

Water vapour escaping through a hole (stoma)

Water is replaced from inner cells.

Water is "pulled" up through xylem.

More water is taken in through root hairs.

STANDING FIRM

Healthy plants usually stand firm and upright. This is because their vacuoles are full of cell sap, and push outwards against the cytoplasm and cell walls. Each cell is described as **turgid**, and the plant is in a state of **turgor**.

A healthy plant

WILTING

In hot or dry conditions, a plant may lose more water than it can take in. The pressure of water in its vacuoles drops to become less than that of the cell walls. This makes the cells limp. They cannot support the plant, so it droops. This state is known as **wilting**.

A wilting plant

In extreme cases, a plant may lose too much water through its leaves, and also through its roots into very dry or mineral-rich soil. Its cell vacuoles then shrink so much that the cytoplasm is pulled away from the cell walls. This state, called **plasmolysis**, may kill the plant unless it receives more water quickly.

A dying plant

LOSING LIQUID

Here you can see water droplets oozing out of tiny holes around the leaf's edge.

If a plant does not lose enough water vapour by transpiration, and root pressure is still pushing water up the stem, the plant may also lose water in liquid form. Droplets are forced out of the plant through tiny holes at the tips or along the edges of leaves. This type of water loss is called **guttation**.

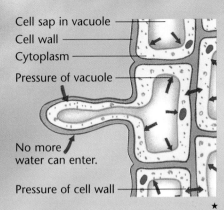

Root cells of a healthy plant

Cell sap in vacuole
Cell wall
Cytoplasm
Pressure of vacuole
No more water can enter.
Pressure of cell wall

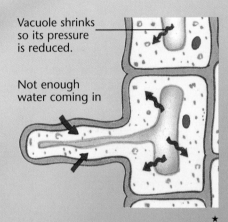

Root cells of a wilting plant

Vacuole shrinks so its pressure is reduced.
Not enough water coming in

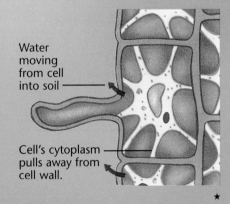

Root cells of a dying plant

Water moving from cell into soil
Cell's cytoplasm pulls away from cell wall.

See for yourself

Water containing blue ink

To see how fluids move inside a plant, put some white flowers, such as carnations, into water containing blue ink. After a few days, their petals will have turned blue. This is because the inky water has been transported around the plants.

The lighter flowers in this picture have been in the dye for one day. The darker flowers have been in the dye for three days.

Internet links

• Go to **www.usborne-quicklinks.com** for a link to the **Microscopy UK Web site** to see a step-by-step guide to fluid transport, with excellent microscope images.

• Go to **www.usborne-quicklinks.com** for a link to **Reeko's Mad Scientist Lab Web site** to find an experiment that demonstrates how capillary action works.

• Go to **www.usborne-quicklinks.com** for a link to the **Osmosis Web pages** where you can read an advanced explanation of fluid transport.

PLANT FOOD

Unlike animals, most plants can make the food that they need. These plants are described as **autotrophic**. The process by which they make food is called **photosynthesis**. A small number of plants do not photosynthesize, but feed on living things. You can find out more about these over the page.

PHOTOSYNTHESIS

Photosynthesis uses water, sunlight, and carbon dioxide from the air. It takes place mainly in a plant's leaves, in the long, column-shaped **palisade cells**.

Palisade cells contain tiny structures called **chloroplasts**. These can move around inside the cell, according to how bright the light is and which direction it is coming from. Chloroplasts contain a green chemical called **chlorophyll** which absorbs the Sun's light energy. This is used to power photosynthesis.

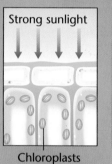

Strong sunlight

Weak sunlight

Chloroplasts

Chloroplasts cluster together

All green plants can make their own food, using sunlight.

The pictures above show how chloroplasts change position to make the best use of available light.

Carbon dioxide from the air is taken in through the surface of the leaves, and the roots take in water from the soil. The carbon dioxide and water are combined using energy taken in from sunlight by chloroplasts. This process produces chemicals called **carbohydrates** (the plant's food), and also oxygen.

Most of the food is used to produce energy for growth. The food that is not needed straight away is stored in the cells as a substance called **starch**.

The process of photosynthesis can be expressed in a word equation like this:

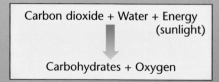

Carbon dioxide + Water + Energy
(sunlight)

↓

Carbohydrates + Oxygen

Section of a leaf

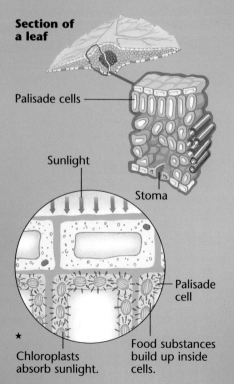

Palisade cells

Sunlight

Stoma

Palisade cell

★

Chloroplasts absorb sunlight.

Food substances build up inside cells.

Photosynthesis in a green plant

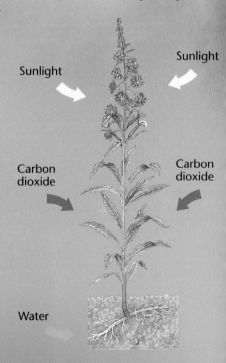

Sunlight

Sunlight

Carbon dioxide

Carbon dioxide

Water

Nitrates and other minerals taken in by the roots are used to build new tissue.

INTERNAL RESPIRATION

Plants get energy from their food in a process called **internal respiration**. In most plants, carbohydrates are combined with oxygen to release energy, carbon dioxide and water.

The process of internal respiration can be expressed in a word equation like this:

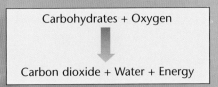

Carbohydrates + Oxygen

Carbon dioxide + Water + Energy

WORKING TOGETHER

The processes of photosynthesis and internal respiration are closely linked. Photosynthesis produces oxygen and carbohydrates, which are both needed for respiration. Respiration produces carbon dioxide and water, which are needed for photosynthesis.

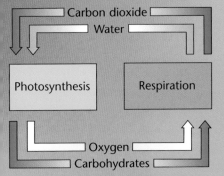

At most times of the day, one of the processes happens at a faster rate than the other. For example, in bright sunshine, photosynthesis happens faster. The plant produces more oxygen and carbohydrates than it can use for respiration. The unused oxygen is given off into the air and the carbohydrates are stored in the plant as starch.

COMPENSATION POINTS

At two points in a 24 hour period, normally at dusk and dawn, the processes of photosynthesis and respiration are exactly balanced. This means that photosynthesis produces just the right amounts of carbohydrates and oxygen for respiration, which produces the right amounts of carbon dioxide and water for photosynthesis. These times are called **compensation points**.

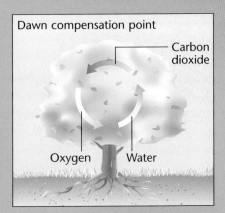

1. At dawn, rates of photosynthesis and respiration are equal.

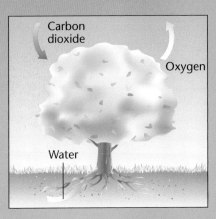

2. During the day the light is bright, so photosynthesis is faster.

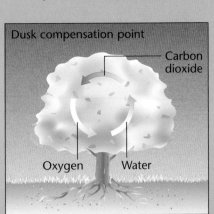

3. At dusk, rates of photosynthesis and respiration are equal.

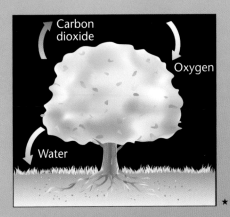

4. At night there is no sunlight, so no photosynthesis takes place.

See for yourself

You can do a simple test to show that sunlight is needed for photosynthesis. Take a houseplant with broad, light-green leaves and fold a piece of paper around one leaf. Secure it with a paper clip. Leave the plant in a sunny place for a few days, then remove the paper. The leaf will have a yellow strip, where it has been unable to photosynthesize.

Internet links

• Go to **www.usborne-quicklinks.com** for links to the **The Greenhouse Web site, Sambal's Science Web site** and the **Photosynthesis Web pages** for a range of information about photosynthesis.

• Go to **www.usborne-quicklinks.com** for a link to the **Kid's World Web site** where you can read a description of how a plant gets its food.

• Go to **www.usborne-quicklinks.com** for a link to the **BrainPop Web site** to watch a movie about photosynthesis.

• Go to **www.usborne-quicklinks.com** for a link to the **Online Biology Book Web site** where you can find out more about the chemistry of photosynthesis.

A small number of plants are **parasites**. This means that they do not make their own food, but live and feed on other living things, called **hosts**. Some parasitic plants attack many different types of plants, and can be harmful to their host.

The dodder plant, for example, attaches itself firmly to its host plant by sinking thread-like structures called **haustoria** into it. Dodder stems then grow rapidly all over the host, which becomes completely covered and eventually dies.

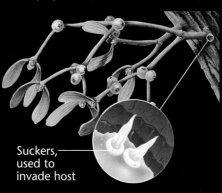

Dodder stem

Host plant

Dodder stems stretch from one plant to another in a hair-like mass.

Some parasites can only live on one host. A Rafflesia plant, for example, can only grow on a particular type of vine. The Rafflesia lives in its host's roots as a mass of tangled threads, causing it little harm.

When conditions are right, the Rafflesia produces a huge, foul-smelling flower, which attracts the flies needed to spread its pollen.

Rafflesia flowers are the largest in the world. They can weigh up to 7kg.

HEMIPARASITES

Plants called **hemiparasites** steal water and minerals but, unlike true parasites, they have green leaves and can therefore also make their own food by photosynthesis*.

Some hemiparasites attach themselves to their host's roots underground. Others, such as common mistletoe, attack them above ground.

Common mistletoe is a hemiparasite found on trees. It grows on branches, and spreads by producing sticky, seed-filled berries that are carried away by birds.

Suckers, used to invade host

* Photosynthesis, 22.

Some organisms feed on dead matter instead of living on a host or making their own food. They are known as **saprotrophic plants** or **saprotrophs**. The main body of most saprotrophs is found underground. Fungi and some orchids are saprotrophic.

The main part of a fungus is a mass of threads. These grow and feed under the ground, where it is dark and damp.

EPIPHYTES

Plants called **epiphytes** make their own food, but grow high up on other plants to catch water and get a better share of the light. Most epiphytes do not harm their host, although some, such as strangler figs, kill their host when they are fully grown.

Development of a strangler fig

Small fig plant starts to grow on a branch. It sends roots down the tree.

Roots start to take water and nutrients from the soil, and fig plant grows rapidly.

Fig plant takes all of host's light, water and nutrients. Host dies and rots away.

MEAT EATERS

Some plants, called **carnivorous plants**, can kill and digest small creatures, such as insects. Carnivorous plants lure their victims into deadly traps using particular smells or colours. Once inside, the insect is dissolved by powerful chemicals called **enzymes**.

Plants that feed in this way usually grow in soil which contains few minerals. They absorb what they need from the bodies of their prey by digesting them.

Pitcher plants, for example, catch animals in their jug-like leaves, called **pitchers**. Insects come to eat sweet nectar, which is made around the rim of the pitcher and under its lid. The insects fall down the pitcher's slippery walls, and die in a pool of liquid.

Lid (keeps rain out of pitcher)

Insects cannot climb back up the pitcher's slippery sides.

Sundews are carnivorous plants. Their leaves have hairs with sticky, gleaming drops at the end. These attract insects, which become trapped. As the insect struggles, the hairs start to curl over, wrapping up their prey tightly. The insect's body is then dissolved into a liquid and digested.

Fly trapped on a sundew leaf

The carnivorous Venus flytrap has pairs of leaves which snap shut like jaws to trap insects or other small animals. The leaves close when sensitive hairs on their surface are disturbed. Once trapped, the prey is slowly dissolved and digested by the plant.

This Venus flytrap will snap shut when the fly lands.

Internet links

• Go to **www.usborne-quicklinks.com** for links to the **Wayne's Word Web site** where you can find excellent information about all kinds of carnivorous and parasitic plants, with photos and illustrations.

• Go to **www.usborne-quicklinks.com** for links to the **International Carnivorous Plant Society Web site** to find an online carnivorous plant museum and answers to many carnivorous plant questions.

• Go to **www.usborne-quicklinks.com** for a link to the **Botanical Society of America Web site** for a detailed and illustrated guide to Venus flytraps.

• Go to **www.usborne-quicklinks.com** for a link to the **Dyra's Nature Study Web site** to follow the life cycle of a Rafflesia flower.

PLANT SENSITIVITY

Vines have thread-like tendrils which are sensitive to touch. This lets them twine around a support.

All living things can react to changes in their environment. This is known as **sensitivity**, or responding to a **stimulus**. Unlike animals, plants do not have a specialized nervous system, but they are still able to react slowly to stimuli such as light, touch and temperature.

PLANT RESPONSE

Most plants respond to a stimulus by growing towards or away from it. This response is called a **tropism**. Growing towards a stimulus is known as a **positive tropism**, and growing away from it is known as a **negative tropism**.

RESPONDING TO LIGHT

Almost all plants react to the amount of light available and the direction from which it is coming. This response is called **phototropism**. For instance, the leaves of most plants turn to face the Sun. This helps them to absorb as much light as possible for photosynthesis*.

The sunflowers below respond to light by turning to face the Sun.

Tropisms are controlled by **auxins**. These are growth hormones (chemicals) made in the plant's cells. Plant stems contain an auxin which collects in cells furthest from the light, causing these areas to grow more quickly. This makes the plant grow towards the light.

Plant growing towards light

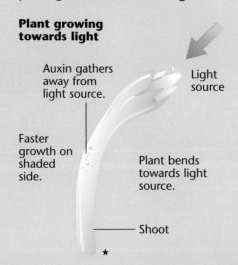

Auxin gathers away from light source.

Light source

Faster growth on shaded side.

Plant bends towards light source.

Shoot

★

GRAVITY AND WATER

All roots respond to the pull of gravity. This is **geotropism**. The roots grow down into the soil to obtain water and minerals. Some roots also show a response to water, called **hydrotropism**. They may grow out sideways if more water lies in that direction.

Plant responding to gravity

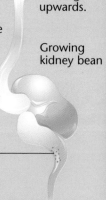

Shoot grows upwards.

The tips of roots and shoots produce growth hormones (auxins) which respond to gravity in different ways.

Growing kidney bean

Auxin gathers here and stimulates cell enlargement.

Auxin gathers here and prevents cell enlargement.

Root grows downwards. ★

* Photosynthesis, 22.

RESPONDING TO TOUCH

Some plants are sensitive to touch. This response, which is known as **haptotropism** or **thigmotropism**, can help a plant in different ways. For example, meat-eating plants trap their food when it touches sensitive parts on their surface (see page 25).

Being able to respond to touch is also important to climbing plants, such as vines. When their thread-like tendrils touch something, it triggers a climbing and twining response.

This sweet pea's touch-sensitive tendrils help it to climb.

In some plants, touch causes a reaction which acts as a defence. For instance, the leaves of a mimosa (nicknamed the "sensitive plant") instantly close and droop when touched. This is because touch causes the pressure of water in its leaf cells to drop.

The leaves of this mimosa close up like fans when they are touched.

Open leaf

Closed leaf

DAY AND NIGHT

Many plants will only grow during periods when light is available for a certain length of time. These periods are called **photoperiods**, and the plant's response is **photoperiodism**.

Long-night plants, such as chrysanthemums, only produce flowers at times of the year when the night is longer than a certain length, called its **critical length**. (These plants are also known as short-day plants.)

Short-night plants, such as larkspur, only produce flowers if the night is shorter than the critical length. (These plants are also known as long-day plants.)

It is thought that there is a growth hormone called **florigen** produced in the leaves, which makes a plant behave like this. When the correct amount of light is available, the florigen sends a "message" telling the plant to produce flowers.

Some plants, such as snapdragons, are described as **night-neutral** or **day-neutral**. Their flowering does not depend on the night's length.

Photoperiodism may be affected by the age of the plant, or the temperature of its surroundings.

Chrysanthemums flower when the nights are long.

Larkspur flowers when the nights are short.

A snapdragon flowers whether the nights are long or short.

See for yourself

Leave a potted plant in a room with one window. Place it a little way from the window and water it as usual. After a few days, you will see that the plant's leaves are leaning towards the window. If you turn the plant around, after a few more days the same thing will have happened. This is because leaves always grow towards the nearest source of light.

Internet links

• Go to **www.usborne-quicklinks.com** for a link to the **Biological Timing Web site** to to see if time of day has an effect on plant movement

• Go to **www.usborne-quicklinks.com** for a link to the **La Trobe University Web site** for a detailed description of various plant responses and the chemicals which control them.

• Go to **www.usborne-quicklinks.com** for a link to the **Ohio State University Web site** for an advanced look at various tropisms.

• Go to **www.usborne-quicklinks.com** for a link to the **Online Biology Book Web site** for information about various plant hormones.

FLOWERING PLANTS

There are over 250,000 different kinds of flowering plants, including grasses, wild flowers, shrubs and trees. Plants which produce flowers are known as **angiosperms**. All flowering plants have certain features in common. For example, they all produce seeds and contain tissue which transports fluid around the plant.

Buttercup ★

Petal

Bud

Unopened petals

Sepal

Carpel (female part)

Receptacle

Stamen (male part)

FLOWERS

Reproduction is the creation of new life. Flowers contain the parts of plants needed for reproduction. These produce male and female sex cells, called **gametes**, which join together to create new plants of the same kind. This type of reproduction is called **sexual reproduction**.

Flowers are made up of many specialized parts. These include petals, stamens (the male parts), and one or more carpels (the female parts). In most plants, the petals are arranged in a circle, around the male and female parts.

Just before a plant blooms, it produces a **bud**, which will eventually develop into a flower. It grows from the expanded tip of a stalk, called the **receptacle**. Buds are surrounded and protected by small, leaf-like **sepals**.

In some plants, such as buttercups, the sepals remain as a ring around the flower after the bud has opened. In others, such as poppies, they wither and fall off.

Petals are delicate, often brightly coloured, and surround the plant's reproductive parts. Many petals are scented or patterned and have areas of cells called **nectaries** at their base. These produce a sweet, sticky liquid called **nectar**, which attracts insects or other animals needed for pollination*.

Nectary at base of a buttercup petal

Poppy ★

Together, a flower's petals are known as the **corolla**

Stamen (male part)

Carpel (female part)

Petal

Sepals have fallen off.

Bud

Unopened petals

Sepal

The petals of these Californian poppies surround their reproductive parts. Their sepals have fallen off.

* Pollination, 30.

MALE PARTS

A flower's male reproductive parts are called **stamens**. Each stamen is made up of a pod-like **anther**, at the end of a long stalk called a **filament**. Anthers contain **pollen sacs**, which split open to release grains of **pollen**, the male reproductive cells.

Male parts of a buttercup

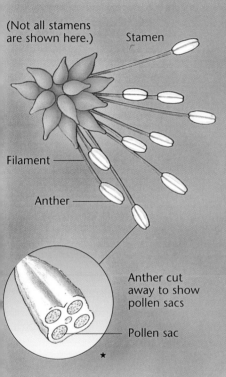

(Not all stamens are shown here.)

Stamen

Filament

Anther

Anther cut away to show pollen sacs

Pollen sac

Pollen grains from different plants may be different sizes and shapes, but they do share some features. For instance, when they are mature, all pollen grains have a hard outer wall, making them very tough.

See for yourself

Look at different types of flowers and, using the pictures on these pages, try to identify their male and female parts.

You may find that not every plant has both parts together in the same flower. They may be on separate flowers or on separate plants.

FEMALE PARTS

A flower's female reproductive part is known as the **carpel** or **pistil**. It is made up of the stigma, style and ovary.

The **stigma** is the top part of a carpel. It has a sticky surface which traps grains of pollen that touch it. The stigma is joined to the ovary by a part of the carpel called the **style**. Each **ovary** holds one or more tiny eggs called **ovules**, which are the female reproductive cells. These develop into seeds after fertilization (see next page).

Female parts of a buttercup

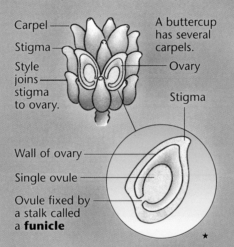

Carpel

Stigma

Style joins stigma to ovary.

A buttercup has several carpels.

Ovary

Stigma

Wall of ovary

Single ovule

Ovule fixed by a stalk called a **funicle**

Some flowers, like the buttercup above, have several carpels clustered together. Others, such as the poppy below, have only one.

Female parts of a poppy

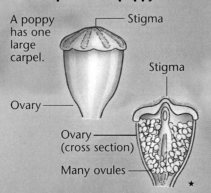

A poppy has one large carpel.

Stigma

Stigma

Ovary

Ovary (cross section)

Many ovules

The styles of many flowers, such as daffodils, are easy to see. In others, such as poppies, the style is very short and almost impossible to see.

MALE AND FEMALE

Buttercups and tulips are examples of **hermaphrodite** plants. This means each flower has both male and female parts.

You can see the female carpel and the male stamens in the centre of this tulip.

Some plants, such as maize, have two types of flowers on one plant: **staminate** flowers, which have only male parts, and **pistillate** flowers, which have only female parts. Plants with flowers of this kind are described as **monoecious**. Other plants, such as holly, have staminate and pistillate flowers on separate plants. They are described as **dioecious**.

Holly has its male and female parts on separate plants. Berries develop from the ovaries of the female plant.

Internet links

• Go to **www.usborne-quicklinks.com** for a link to **Ross Koning's Web site** to learn about types of pollen dispersal.

• Go to **www.usborne-quicklinks.com** for a link to the **Wayne's Word Web site** to learn about diversity in flowering plants.

• Go to **www.usborne-quicklinks.com** for a link to the **Online Biology Book Web site** to take a detailed look at flowering plants.

• Go to **www.usborne-quicklinks.com** for a link to the **Gardening Web site** to use a searchable plant encyclopedia.

FERTILIZATION

In order for a flowering plant to reproduce, the male cell (pollen) and the female cell (ovule) need to join together. This is called **fertilization**.

When a pollen grain lands on the stigma of a plant of the same type, it forms a **pollen tube**. This grows down into the ovary and enters an ovule through a tiny hole called a **micropyle**. This process is called **pollination**.

Cross section of poppy ovary

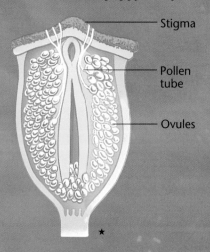

- Stigma
- Pollen tube
- Ovules

★

A pollen grain contains two male nuclei*. These travel down the pollen tube and join with the contents of the ovule. One forms a **zygote** – the first cell of a new organism. The other forms a layer of protective, nourishing tissue called the **endosperm**. Together these make a seed, and the ovary grows to become a fruit. After fertilization, the plant no longer needs the rest of its flower parts, so they wither and die.

* Nucleus, 8.

POLLINATION METHODS

Pollen may be carried from plant to plant by wind, water or animals. When pollen from one plant pollinates another plant of the same kind, it is described as **cross-pollination**. If the grains land on a different type of plant, they don't produce pollen tubes, so pollination can't take place.

Some types of plants are able to pollinate themselves. This is called **self-pollination**. For instance, a bee orchid tries to attract a certain type of bee, by looking and smelling like the female of its species. But if no bees come, the plant's stamens bend over and transfer pollen to its own stigma.

Unlike many flowers, a bee orchid does not produce sweet nectar. It attracts bees by looking and smelling like a female bee.

ANIMAL POLLINATION

Flowers have various ways of attracting animals to carry their pollen. Most have brightly coloured petals or sweet scents which attract insects, birds or bats. Many also produce a sweet liquid called nectar, or extra pollen, on which the animals feed. Some have patterns on the petals called **nectar guides**. These lead the insect into the middle of the flower, where the pollen or nectar can be found.

Nectar guides in the middle of these pansies lead insects to the nectar.

Plants pollinated by animals tend to produce spiky pollen grains. When an animal visits a plant, pollen grains stick to its body. The animal may then transfer these to another flower.

Thousands of tiny pollen grains are being shed from stamens in the middle of this flower.

WIND POLLINATION

Wind-pollinated plants rely on the wind to scatter their pollen. They do not need to attract animals, so their flowers are usually unscented, with very small petals and sepals. Some have their male and female parts on separate plants. The male parts hang outside the flowers, allowing their pollen to be scattered more easily.

Pollen from these birch tree catkins is scattered by the wind.

Plants which are pollinated by the wind produce huge amounts of pollen. This increases the chances of some landing on female flowers nearby. The pollen grains are usually smooth and light, allowing them to glide easily through the air.

See for yourself

If you have a garden, you can plant flowers to attract certain types of animals. For instance, butterflies tend to visit plants with purple or yellow flowers, such as buddleia or sedum. Bees are attracted to flowers with a strong scent, such as lavender.

Pollen sticks to this butterfly's body as it feeds from a daisy.

FLOWER SHAPES

The shapes of many flowers help them to transfer pollen onto an animal. For example, the petals of some flowers are shaped like a bell. Animals such as the hummingbird on the right hover beneath the flower, and reach in to feed on the nectar. As they do so, pollen from the stamens sticks to them.

Lipped flowers, such as sage flowers, have paired petals. A bee lands on the lower petal to drink nectar from within the flower. As it does so, the stamens, which hang down from the top lip, transfer pollen onto its body.

As the bee lands on this sage flower's lower "lip" to drink nectar, pollen is brushed onto its body.

Pollen rubs off on the hummingbird's head as it feeds with its long beak.

Most flowers have ways of keeping their pollen safe until they are visited by a certain kind of animal. For instance, evening primrose flowers remain closed all day. They open up at night, when the moths which pollinate them become active. Many flowers close up when it begins to rain, to keep their pollen dry.

Internet links

• Go to www.usborne-quicklinks.com for a link to the **Enchanted Learning Web site** to discover which plants to grow if you want to attract butterflies into your garden.

• Go to www.usborne-quicklinks.com for a link to the **Microscopy UK Web site** to take a close-up look at a dandelion.

• Go to www.usborne-quicklinks.com for a link to the **BrainPop Web site** to watch a movie about pollination.

• Go to www.usborne-quicklinks.com for a link to the **Smithsonian Institute Web site** to read an essay on pollination.

• Go to www.usborne-quicklinks.com for a link to the **Canadian Botanical Conservation Network Web site** for lots of useful flowering plant information.

SEEDS AND FRUIT

Fertilization in flowering plants leads to the production of a **seed**. Each seed contains a new developing plant and a store of food. Seeds are kept in a part of the plant called a **fruit**. When the seeds are ready, they are scattered and can grow into new plants if conditions are right.

INSIDE A SEED

Seeds are protected by a tough coat called a **testa**. Each has a mark called a **hilum** on its surface, showing where the ovule* was joined to the ovary*. The tiny hole (micropyle) through which the pollen grain entered the ovule can also still be seen. It lets in water.

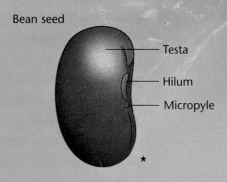

Bean seed

— Testa

— Hilum

— Micropyle

★

The developing plant inside a seed is known as an **embryo**. It has two parts: the **plumule**, which will develop into the first shoot, and the **radicle**, which will be the first root of the new plant.

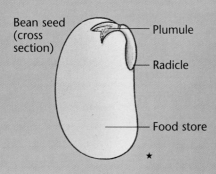

Bean seed (cross section)

— Plumule

— Radicle

— Food store

★

This orange fruit protects the seeds of the orange tree. Its flesh is made up of tiny hairs, each one swollen with juice.

Orange seed (pip) —

TYPES OF FRUIT

Fruit protect the seeds they carry and help them to spread to a place where they can grow. Most fruit develop from a plant's ovary*. These are known as **true fruit**. Some, such as strawberries, develop from the receptacle* and the ovary. They are **false fruit**. Fruits can also be described as succulent or dry.

SUCCULENT FRUIT

Fruit with thick, fleshy layers that are often tasty to eat are known as **succulent fruit**. There are various kinds.

Succulent fruit with a single, hard-cased seed in the middle are called **drupes**. Plums and cherries are drupes.

Plum

Succulent fruit that contain many seeds are called **berries**. Oranges are berries. Fruit with a thick, fleshy outer layer and a core, with the seeds contained in a capsule, are false fruit called **pomes**.

Apples are pomes.

Raspberries and blackberries are examples of **aggregate fruit** or **compound fruit**. They form from many ovaries in one flower. Each fruit is made up of fleshy beads called **drupelets**, each containing a single seed.

Blackberries

* Ovary, Ovule, 29; Receptacle, 28.

DRY FRUIT

Dry fruit are dry cases that hold the seeds until they are ripe. There are several types. The main ones are described below.

Nuts are dry fruit with only one seed surrounded by a hard shell. Acorns and walnuts are nuts.

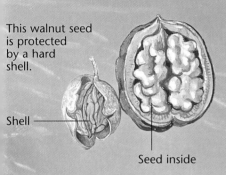

This walnut seed is protected by a hard shell.

Shell

Seed inside

Achenes are small, dry fruit with only one seed. An achene with papery wings, for example an ash or sycamore fruit, is called a **samara** or **key fruit**. Some achenes, such as ash achenes, grow in bunches.

This sycamore fruit has wings which help it to float on the wind.

A dry fruit with seeds attached to its inside wall is known as a **legume** or **pod**. It splits along its length to open. The fruit of the pea plant are pods. The peas are the seeds.

This pea pod has been split open to show the seeds attached inside it.

A **grain**, also called a **caryopsis** or a **kernel**, is a small dry fruit whose wall has fused with the seed coat. Wheat and barley are examples of plants with many grains.

The fruit of the wheat plant is called grain. Each stalk carries many grains.

CONES

The seeds of conifer trees are contained in **cones**, not fruit. These develop from the female flowers (conifers have male and female flowers). After pollination* the scales harden and close.

Atlas cedar cone

When the seeds are ripe and the weather is warm and dry, the scales of the cones open. The seeds flutter out on papery wings. Most cones stay on the tree for a year. Others take two years to ripen, and some remain long after the seeds have been dropped.

See for yourself

Look at as many different types of fruit as you can find. Notice whether they are succulent or dry fruit, and the number of seeds they contain. If you find a cone, you could make it open by placing it on a radiator. If you put it in a damp place, its scales will close up.

Internet links

• Go to www.usborne-quicklinks.com for a link to the **Wayne's Word Web site** where you can find detailed information about many different types of fruit, nut and berry, with links to photos and related articles.

• Go to www.usborne-quicklinks.com for a link to the **Missouri Botanical Garden Web site** where you can choose from a list of tropical fruit to find pictures and essential information, including how the fruit is eaten.

• Go to www.usborne-quicklinks.com for a link to the **Fruit Pages Web site** to find a searchable fruit resource where you can read information about the different types of fruit, see the fruit of the month, take a fruit survey and more.

SCATTERING SEEDS

Before seeds start to grow into new plants, they are usually carried away from the parent plant. This is called **dispersal**, and it helps to stop new plants from competing with their parents for space, light and water. Some seeds, such as peas, burst out of the fruit while it is still attached to the parent plant.

Ripe pea fruit explode and fling out their seeds.

Other seeds are carried away from their parent plant inside the fruit. Seeds can be spread by several methods, including by animals, water and wind.

ANIMAL DISPERSAL

Some seeds are tasty to animals or are held inside tempting, fleshy fruit. Animals eat them, and the seeds pass out in their droppings. Some animals, such as squirrels and jays, store away fruit and seeds. Sometimes they put them in a place that is ideal for new plants to sprout.

Not all animal-dispersed fruit are eaten. Some, such as those of burdock or goosegrass, have hooks on them which catch in the fur of passing animals. A fruit can be carried a long way from its parent plant before it falls off.

Burdock fruit have hooks that catch on animals' fur.

WATER DISPERSAL

Seeds or fruit that are dispersed by water, such as coconuts, have waterproof shells. Coconuts contain the seeds of coconut palm trees. They float in rivers or on seas until they are washed up on shore. Some have travelled up to 2,000km on ocean currents before reaching land.

The coconut fruit is held inside a large, waterproof outer shell, seen here.

WIND DISPERSAL

Fruit or seeds which are dispersed by the wind are very light. Some seeds, such as those of sycamore trees, are held in fruit with papery wings. Others, such as dandelions, have fruit with hairs that catch the wind.

Sycamore fruit, each containing two seeds

Parachute ———

Fruit with seed inside

Each dandelion seed is held inside a fruit attached to a parachute of very fine hairs. The lightest breeze catches the parachute and pulls the fruit off the parent plant.

Dandelion fruit can be carried many miles by the wind.

GERMINATION

When conditions are right, a seed will begin to grow into a new plant. This is called **germination**. To germinate, a seed needs warmth, oxygen and water. The seed absorbs water and starts to swell. Its testa splits open and the first shoot and root (the **plumule** and **radicle**) grow.

Germinating pea seed

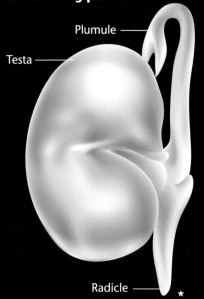

Plumule

Testa

Radicle ⭐

Many seeds that are scattered do not start to grow right away. Seeds that lie inactive for a long time before germinating are described as **dormant**.

The first leaves to grow are called **cotyledons** or **seed leaves**. They are often a different shape from later, true leaves. Some plants, such as grasses and tulips, have only one cotyledon. They are known as **monocotyledons**. Those with two cotyledons, such as peas, are **dicotyledons**.

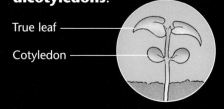

True leaf

Cotyledon

The young plant, called a **seedling**, lives off the food stored in its seed until it grows leaves. It then starts to make its own food by photosynthesis*. It grows and eventually flowers, ready to begin the cycle again.

See for yourself

To germinate seeds such as dried kidney beans or lentils, place them on a piece of paper towel in a saucer, and water them thoroughly every day. After a few days, they will have sprouted. If you like, you can then plant them in small pots.

GERMINATION TYPES

There are two main types of germination. In **hypogeal germination** the cotyledons stay below the ground inside the testa, and the plumule is the only part to come above the ground. Peas germinate in this way.

Germination of a pea plant

Cotyledons stay inside testa below ground.

Plumule comes above ground.

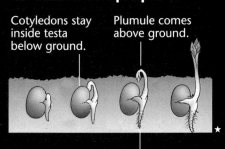

Radicle grows down.

In **epigeal germination**, the cotyledons appear above the ground, below the first true leaves. Beans germinate in this way.

Germination of a bean plant

Plumule comes above ground.

Testa falls off.

True leaves

Cotyledons

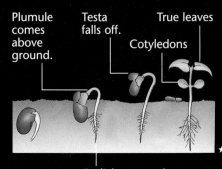

Radicle grows down.

Internet links

• Go to **www.usborne-quicklinks.com** for a link to the **Wayne's Word Web site** to discover how some seeds and fruit are dispersed by the wind and the sea.

• Go to **www.usborne-quicklinks.com** for a link to **Ross Koning's Web site** for a seed structure and germination essay.

• Go to **www.usborne-quicklinks.com** for a link to the **Plants and Our Environment Web site** for a simple look at seed structure.

• Go to **www.usborne-quicklinks.com** for a link to the **Shades of Green Web site** for lots about seeds, nuts and fruit.

*Photosynthesis, 22.

NEW PLANTS FROM OLD

As well as making seeds which grow into new plants, many plants can reproduce by a process in which part of the plant develops into a new one. This method, called **vegetative reproduction** or **vegetative propagation**, is a type of asexual reproduction, which means it does not involve a male and female sex cell. Some of the different plant parts that can grow into new plants are described here.

Each crocus has grown from a swollen stem called a corm.

BULBS

Plants such as garlic and tulips grow from bulbs. A **bulb** is a short, thick, underground stem surrounded by scaly leaves that are swollen with food. It stays alive over winter when the rest of the plant has died. Some bulbs can reproduce asexually by sprouting extra bulbs on the side.

See for yourself

Garlic bulbs are **composite bulbs**. This means that each swollen leaf, called a **clove**, can grow into a garlic plant.

Try planting a few cloves in a pot of potting compost, with the rounded end down. Keep them watered. After about two weeks, shoots of new garlic plants should appear.

Garlic bulb

CORMS

A **corm** is a short, thick stem base that is swollen with food. It can sprout extra corms each year.

Crocus corms

RUNNERS

Some plants, such as spider plants and strawberry plants, can reproduce by forming long side shoots called **runners** or **stolons**.

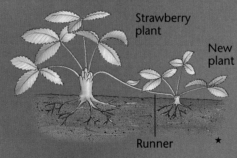

Strawberry plant

New plant

Runner ★

When the runners touch the ground, they develop roots of their own, and start to grow into new plants. At first the new plant is fed by the parent, but once it can live on its own, the runner rots away.

Each clove of garlic can grow into a new plant.

RHIZOMES

Many plants grow from thick stems called **rhizomes** which grow horizontally underground. A rhizome produces roots along its length and also buds from which new shoots grow. Ferns, mint, irises and many grasses are plants that produce rhizomes.

TUBERS

A number of plants produce offspring from swollen underground stems called **tubers**. These develop from shoots which grow into the soil. Food is stored in the tuber. In winter the parent plant dies, but the tubers develop into new plants the following year.

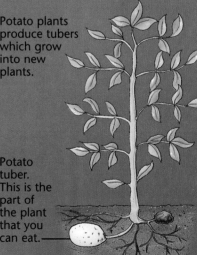
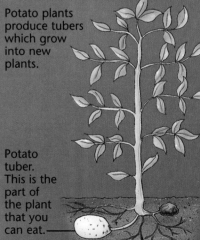

Potato plants produce tubers which grow into new plants.

Potato tuber. This is the part of the plant that you can eat.

★

Tulips like these grow from bulbs. Each year, market gardens provide thousands of tulips for the flower industry.

SPEED AND QUALITY

Vegetative reproduction produces new plants much more quickly than they can grow from seed. Also, the new plants are identical to the parent plant. Farmers and market gardeners often make use of a plant's ability to reproduce vegetatively. As well as producing more plants, they know that the new plants will be the same quality as the original plant.

Growers have also developed methods of removing parts from a plant to grow new plants. These are examples of **artificial propagation** as, left to themselves, plants do not usually reproduce in these ways.

Some varieties of fruit, such as this navel orange, do not have seeds. They can only be grown by artificial propagation methods.

TAKING CUTTINGS

One common method of artificial propagation is **cutting**. This involves taking a piece such as a side stem or leaf (known as the cutting) off a plant and planting it in soil where it grows into a new plant. The cutting may need to stand in water for a while to develop new roots before being planted in soil.

Growing a plant from a cutting

A piece of plant is cut from the parent plant.

The cutting is placed in water until roots begin to grow.

The cutting is replanted in soil, where it will grow into a new plant.

African violet plants can be grown from leaf cuttings.

MICROPROPAGATION

Scientists can grow new plants from just a few cells taken from a meristem (growth area) of a plant. The cells are placed on a gel that contains chemicals which make the cells divide. Groups of cells are then moved to a second gel which contains growth chemicals that make the cells grow into shoots. This method, called **micropropagation**, can create hundreds of identical plants from one parent plant.

Internet links

• Go to **www.usborne-quicklinks.com** for a link to **Ross Koning's Web site** to find detailed information about natural and artificial propagation.

• Go to **www.usborne-quicklinks.com** for a link to the **Potato Then & Now Web site** to read about the biology and history of the potato by clicking on "science & tech".

• Go to **www.usborne-quicklinks.com** for a link to the **Color Blends Web site** where you can discover the fascinating history of the tulip.

• Go to **www.usborne-quicklinks.com** for a link to the **Wayne's Word Web site** for information on root vegetables.

WATER PLANTS

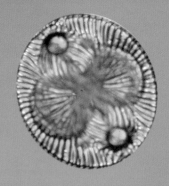

This is a microscopic water plant called a diatom.

Most plants grow on land, but there are also many aquatic plants – plants specially adapted to live in water. These are known as **hydrophytes**. They range from microscopic plants, which are found in groups of several million, to huge flowering plants over a metre across.

A WATERY LIFESTYLE

Water plants are either emergent or submergent. **Emergent** plants, such as reed mace, grow well in very wet soils, or in soils which spend a lot of time covered in water. Most or all of their stems and leaves can be seen above the surface of the water.

Reed mace can often be seen growing out of the water by a river bank.

Submergent plants, such as water lilies, grow beneath the surface of the water. However, some of their parts, for instance large leaves, may float on the surface. Unless they are free-floating, their roots, or root-like parts, anchor them to the ground beneath the water.

Free-floating submergent plants, such as duckweed, are not attached to anything. They are found in large numbers in calm, sheltered water.

This duckweed floats freely on the water's surface.

SPECIAL FEATURES

Water-living plants have a number of special features. For instance, most underwater leaves, unlike leaves of other plants, do not have a waxy waterproof coating. This is because the whole leaf surface is needed for exchanging gases between the plant and the water. Many water plants also have very different leaves above and below the surface.

Above the water's surface, water crowfoot has broad, flat leaves.

Under the water, its leaves are thin and finely divided.

Some submergent plants develop gaps between the cells in their stems and leaves. These gaps trap air which helps the parts to float.

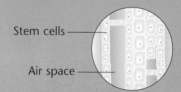

Stem cells

Air space

A water lily's stem and roots grow under water.

Diatoms, like these, are a type of algae.

Each diatom is made up of two halves, which fit together like a lid on a box.

ALGAE

Algae form a large group of plants which have a very simple structure. Most types of algae are found in water, but they can grow in any suitably damp conditions, including in soil, on rocks, and even on living things.

One of the simplest types of algae are microscopic **diatoms**. Most are made up of a single cell, with a hard, glassy case. Each species of diatom has a differently patterned case.

Microscopic algae never have roots, stems or leaves, and don't contain true vascular tissue*. They can reproduce quickly and, like most plants, make their own food using the Sun's energy. Algae are an important source of food for many water creatures.

Pigments, 19; Vascular tissue, 12.

SEAWEEDS

Seaweeds are types of many-celled algae. Most seaweeds have root-like **holdfasts** at their base, which anchor them to solid objects, such as rocks. Some have bubble-like **air bladders**, which keep them afloat. A seaweed's leaves, called **fronds**, often contain pigments* which allow them to take in light at different water depths.

Examples of seaweeds

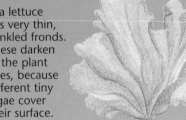

Sea lettuce has very thin, crinkled fronds. These darken as the plant ages, because different tiny algae cover their surface.

Edible dulse grows in deep pools. The red pigment in its fronds helps it to capture light under water.

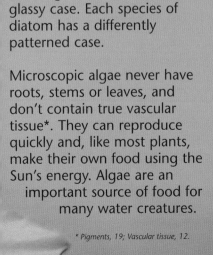

Knotted wrack has long fronds, which contain pockets of air called air bladders.

STUDYING ALGAE

Scientists study the types and numbers of algae in a water sample to find out how clean it is. Single-celled, freshwater algae called **desmids** are generally found growing in clean water.

Some types of algae, though, reproduce rapidly in water which contains high levels of nitrates (chemicals found in some fertilizers and sewage). This is called **eutrophication**. These algae use up oxygen that other living things in the water need, eventually killing them.

Eutrophication is mostly caused by sewage-dumping and by fertilizer being washed from the soil into the water.

Blue-green algae (called cyanobacteria) are starting to cover this polluted lake.

See for yourself

If you visit the coast, look for seaweed of different colours and textures. You may find it in rock pools, or washed up on the shore. Look for features like air bladders or a holdfast.

Internet links

• Go to **www.usborne-quicklinks.com** for a link to the **Evergreen Project Web site** for information on "Aquatic Plants".

• Go to **www.usborne-quicklinks.com** for a link to the **Microscopy UK Web site** to see close-up pictures of tiny water plants by clicking on "Diatoms" or "Desmids".

• Go to **www.usborne-quicklinks.com** for a link to the **Wayne's Word Web site** for photos of algae and diatoms.

• Go to **www.usborne-quicklinks.com** for a link to the **Aquatic Environments Web site** for a look at aquatic plants.

FLOWERLESS PLANTS

Liverworts, mosses, ferns, algae* and horsetails* are known as flowerless plants. They do not produce flowers or seeds, and in many cases reproduce at least some of the time by **asexual reproduction**. This is a type of reproduction in which only one parent is needed to produce a new living thing identical to itself. Many scientists believe that these plants were among the very first types of land plants on the Earth.

These paired horn-shaped clubs contain reproductive cells called spores.

The leaves of this stag's horn club moss are packed tightly around the base of the stem.

LIVERWORTS

Liverworts are low-growing plants that live in damp places on soil or rocks. They do not have true roots, stems or leaves. The main part of a liverwort is called the **thallus**. It is held in the ground by simple root-like growths called **rhizoids**.

Liverworts do not contain vascular tissue* for transporting fluids. They also do not have a waterproof outer layer. This means that they can absorb all the water they need, but are also more likely to dry out.

MOSSES

Mosses are low-growing plants that live in damp, shady places, for example on walls, rocks and tree trunks. Like liverworts, they do not have vascular tissue*. Instead, they absorb large amounts of water through their many tiny leaf-like structures, which are only one cell thick.

If conditions become too dry, the moss leaves curl up, shrivel, and turn brown. They remain inactive until conditions are damp enough for them to grow again.

The Mnium moss below grows on damp rocks and in shady woods.

CLUB MOSSES

Club mosses grow along the ground. They are not mosses at all, but are distantly related to ferns. They have narrow, scale-like leaves packed densely around stems that contain vascular tissue.

Club mosses get their name from their club-shaped growths called **strobili**, which contain reproductive cells called spores.

The tiny capsules on these moss stalks are called **sporangia**. They contain spores (reproductive cells).

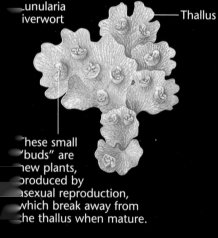

Lunularia liverwort

Thallus

These small "buds" are new plants, produced by asexual reproduction, which break away from the thallus when mature.

The moss absorbs large amounts of water through thousands of tiny leaves.

*Algae, 39; Horsetails, 53; Vascular tissue, 12.

FERNS

There are over 10,000 species of ferns. They grow in damp, shady places all over the world. Unlike mosses and liverworts, they have true leaves, stems and roots, with well-developed vascular tissue. This helps them to survive in drier conditions, and also to grow taller to get a better share of the light.

Most ferns have horizontal stems called rhizomes* that grow underground. Leaves known as **fronds** push out of the earth in tight coils which then unfurl. Fronds are different shapes depending on the type of fern.

This hart's-tongue fern has solid, leathery fronds.

Bracken fronds are made up of many leaflets.

Wall rue ferns have delicate fronds.

These brown specks are spore sacs (sori) on the underside of a fern frond.

REPRODUCTION

Most flowerless plants go through a two-stage reproduction known as **alternation of generations**. In this, a type of asexual reproduction alternates with true sexual reproduction, involving male and female sex cells. At other times, the plants may reproduce by asexual reproduction alone, for instance by producing new bud-like plants called **gemmae**.

The first stage of alternation of generations is sexual. The plant is called a **gametophyte**, because it produces male and female sex cells (gametes). A male cell travels through water to a female cell, and they join and grow into a plant body called a **sporophyte**. Mosses produce gametophytes and sporophytes on the same plant, but in liverworts, ferns and most algae they are on separate plants.

The second, asexual stage is called **sporulation**. The sporophyte produces reproductive cells called **spores**. Ripe spores are scattered, and grow into new gametophytes if they land in suitable conditions.

Fern spores develop in tiny sacs called **sori**. These usually grow in clusters on the underside of the fern's fronds. The scattered spores grow into flat, often heart-shaped gametophytes called **prothalli**.

Life cycle of a fern

Gametophyte (called prothallus) with male and female cells

Spores scatter and form new gametophytes.

Male and female cells join together.

Sporophyte with spores

See for yourself

You may see small mosses growing on walls or on stones in a garden. Look closely at their texture and shape. If you live near a wooded area or even a garden centre, you may also find some ferns. Look for spore sacs on the undersides of their leaves.

Internet links

• Go to **www.usborne-quicklinks.com** for a link to the **Microscopy UK Web site** where you can find a clear explanation of alternation of generations in ferns, with helpful interactive photographs for reference.

• Go to **www.usborne-quicklinks.com** for a link to the **Microscopy UK Web site** where you can find an informative article on mosses and liverworts, with fascinating close-up images.

• Go to **www.usborne-quicklinks.com** for a link to the **Wayne's Word Web site** where you can discover pages containing images of mosses, ferns and many other different flowerless plants, with short descriptions.

• Go to **www.usborne-quicklinks.com** for a link to the **Natural Perspective Web site** where you can read a clearly written introduction to mosses and similar plants, complete with photographs.

* Rhizomes, 36; Vascular tissue, 12.

FUNGI

Fungi are simple, plant-like organisms that never flower and do not have true leaves, stems or roots. They grow in damp, dark places, and do not contain the green chlorophyll needed to make their own food. Instead, they feed on either living things or dead matter. Moulds and yeast are types of fungi.

The mould on this lemon is a type of simple fungus.

STRUCTURE OF FUNGI

The main part of most fungi, called the **mycelium**, is found underground. It is a mass of tiny thread-like structures called **hyphae**, which spread out in the soil. These absorb food substances from dead matter or living roots in the soil. Fungi which live on roots are called **mycorrhizae**.

Mycelium

To reproduce, some of the hyphae pack densely together to form button-like growths. These push up through the soil and grow into **fruiting bodies**.

Growth of a fruiting body

Protective outer layer called a **veil**

Inner veil joins cap to stalk.

Cap

Stalk

Cap expands, and outer layer splits.

Remains of outer veil

Expanding cap

Stalk grows taller. Cap opens out, revealing thin, flat **gills**.

Fruiting body

Gills

Like mosses and ferns, fungi reproduce by producing tiny cells called spores. Fruiting bodies contain millions of spores. When the spores are ready, they are released and scattered by the wind. If they land in suitable conditions, they grow into new fungi.

The fruiting bodies of fungi grow and die very rapidly, but the spores and mycelium can continue to live underground for many years.

Fruiting body of a fungus

MOULDS AND MILDEWS

Moulds and **mildews** are simple fungi which do not produce large fruiting bodies. They grow in warm, damp and dark places, feeding on living or once-living matter, such as paper and wood.

You might see moulds or mildews in your own home or garden. For example, the small blue spots and green furry patches that grow on old bread or fruit are types of mould. Mildews often look like powdery white or black patches. They grow in damp areas, such as bathroom ceilings. Some grow on plants – roses, for example.

The flattened gills of this fungus have opened out to shed its spores.

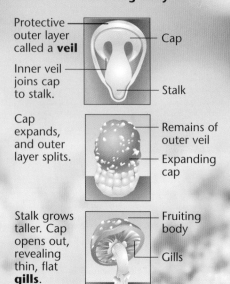

This sulphur shelf fungus is a saprotroph. It lives and feeds on the wood of dead trees.

FUNGI FEEDING

Fungi that feed on dead matter are called **saprotrophs**. Dead matter contains useful substances such as carbon and nitrates. As they feed, fungi release powerful chemicals called **enzymes** which break down their food into simple substances.

Some substances are absorbed by the fungi, but others are returned to the soil, where they are used again by plants and animals. In this way, the fungi play an important part in the carbon and nitrogen cycles*.

Fungi that feed on living things are called **parasites**. Some are good for the plants that they feed on, providing them with water and minerals. This is called a **symbiotic relationship**.

See for yourself

You can look at spores by cutting the stalk off an ordinary cooking mushroom, and placing the cap on a piece of white paper. Cover it with an upturned bowl and leave it overnight. When you remove the bowl and mushroom cap, you will see that the mushroom has released its spores in a pattern on the paper.

Spore print

HELP AND HARM

Some kinds of fungi are useful to people. For instance, a medicine called **penicillin**, which kills the bacteria that cause various diseases, is made from a particular mould. The blue veins in some cheeses are also made from similar moulds. A single-celled fungus called **yeast** is used in bread-making and brewing some alcoholic drinks.

Bread, wine and beer are made using the fungus yeast.

Many fungi can harm living things. Some, for instance, produce fruiting bodies that are highly poisonous. Others, such as the mould which causes Dutch elm disease, grow on plants and slowly kill them. Some fungi can also grow on animals' bodies. For instance, athlete's foot and ringworm are human skin conditions caused by fungi.

This beetle has a fungus feeding on its body.

Internet links

• Go to **www.usborne-quicklinks.com** for a link to the **University of Michigan Web site** to discover fun facts about fungi.

• Go to **www.usborne-quicklinks.com** for a link to the **University of Toronto Web site** for mould and related topics.

• Go to **www.usborne-quicklinks.com** for a link to the **Natural Perspective Web site** for many pages about fungi.

• Go to **www.usborne-quicklinks.com** for a link to the **University of California Web site** to find a detailed study of fungi.

• Go to **www.usborne-quicklinks.com** for a link to the **Electron Microscopy Gallery Web site** to see incredible microscope images of fungi and mould.

• Go to **www.usborne-quicklinks.com** for a link to the **Online Biology Book Web site** for an in-depth look at mould.

*Carbon cycle, Nitrogen cycle, 50.

FIGHTING FOR SURVIVAL

Every living thing in nature struggles to survive. Most plants are threatened by animals and people, as well as by other plants, and may have to live in difficult conditions. Plants survive by adapting to life in different environments, and competing successfully with other living things.

NATURAL SELECTION

Over time, some plants develop features which help them to survive in particular conditions. Plants with helpful features are more likely to survive and reproduce. Plants without these features often die out. This process is called **natural selection**.

COASTAL PLANTS

The seashore is an example of an environment where conditions can be harsh. There is little firm soil or fresh water, and strong, salty winds often blow. Even so, some plants have adapted to life in these surroundings.

For instance, when a sand dune first forms, only grasses grow there. Their roots form a network which helps to bind together the loose, sandy ground, eventually creating a kind of soil that other types of flowering plants can grow in.

Grasses growing on sand dunes help to make the ground firmer.

Shingle beaches are made up of small rock fragments, mixed with sand. Only plants with long or sprawling roots, which hold the plant firmly in the shingle, can live in these areas. Long roots also help the plant to reach supplies of fresh water deep under the ground.

Yellow horned poppies are anchored firmly in the shingle by their long roots.

Areas called **salt marshes** form where a river joins the sea. Their soil is **saline** (salty), which means that most plants are not able to grow in it.

A group of plants known as **halophytes** can survive in saline areas. Some need salt in order to grow. Others are adapted to remove salt from water that they take in. For example, some halophytes have **salt bladders** on the surface of their leaves. These bladders burst to release salt. Other halophytes store the salt in old leaves, which they later shed.

Sea asters grow best in salty conditions.

This yucca is a desert plant. It has narrow, tough leaves, which lose little water.

DESERT PLANTS

Plants which grow in very dry areas, such as deserts, are called **xerophytes**. There are many ways in which they make the most of the limited water supply. For example, some have very small leaves, or needle-like leaves called **spines**, which lose very little water. Most desert plants have specially adapted cells which store water.

These cacti store water in their thick, fleshy stems.

PROTECTION

Plants are constantly under threat from animals that want to eat them. Some plants have special features which protect them from hungry animals and other dangers. These features are known as **protective adaptations**.

Some plants, such as this dog rose, have sharp thorns or prickles which make them difficult for animals to eat.

Thorn

Tiny hairs on this nettle's leaves release a stinging chemical when they are touched.

Many plants are damaged by hungry insect grubs, such as caterpillars. These hatch out of eggs laid on the plant's leaves.

Some passion flower vines protect themselves from this threat by developing small growths which look like butterfly eggs. Butterflies are less likely to lay eggs on a plant which looks as if it already has some on it. Only a small number of real eggs are laid on the plant, so it is attacked by few caterpillars.

This butterfly thinks the false eggs are real. It will not lay its own eggs near them.

False egg

Passion flower vine

ROCK PLANTS

Plants which live on the surface of rocks are called **lithophytes**. They are mostly found on walls, cliff-faces or mountainsides. Lithophytes usually have special roots which anchor them to rocks.

Mosses are one of the few types of plants that can survive on rocks.

Some types of plants use tricks and disguises to keep themselves safe. For instance, living stone plants have adapted to blend in perfectly with pebbles on the ground. Animals mistake them for real stones, and do not try to eat them. This type of disguise is called **camouflage**.

Living stones grow on the ground. They look like pebbles.

Internet links

• Go to www.usborne-quicklinks.com for a link to the **PBS Nature Web site** to discover how some plants and seeds have adapted to survive in their environments.

• Go to www.usborne-quicklinks.com for a link to the **Desert USA Web site** to learn about plant survival in the desert.

• Go to www.usborne-quicklinks.com for a link to the **Geo-Globe Web site** to play a plant adaptation game by clicking on "Geo-adapt".

• Go to www.usborne-quicklinks.com for a link to the **Living Earth Web site** to find out how rainforest plants protect themselves.

• Go to www.usborne-quicklinks.com for a link to the **Evergreen Web site** to learn about plants in different ecosystems.

PLANT LIFESTYLES

The way a plant grows and reproduces depends on many things, such as climate, soil and weather conditions. Some plants live in areas where growth is impossible for some parts of the year, so they grow quickly and reproduce many times when conditions are right. Others may grow one year and reproduce the next. Each year in a plant's life is described as a single **growth season**.

These blue daisies are perennials. They bloom year after year.

ANNUALS

Flowering plants that live and die within a single year are called **annuals**. The entire process of growth, flowering and seed production may take place in as little as a few weeks. Annual plants have usually bloomed and died by the end of the summer. Their seeds remain inactive during the winter, ready to grow into new plants when spring comes.

This lobelia grows, flowers and dies within a single year.

BIENNIALS

Some flowering plants take two years to complete their life cycle. They are called **biennials**. During the first year, they grow and store up food. In the second year, the plant grows taller, blooms and produces seeds. After this, the entire plant dies.

Wallflowers grow and store food in one year, then flower and die in the next.

PERENNIALS

Plants that live for many years are called **perennials**. There are two types. **Herbaceous perennials** lose all the parts that are above ground each winter. Their roots become swollen with food and remain inactive until new shoots sprout from them the following spring.

Shrubs and trees are **woody perennials**. They may lose some parts, such as leaves, during the winter, but their stems or trunks stay alive, growing thicker each year.

TREE LIFESTYLES

Trees can be divided into two categories: deciduous and evergreen. **Deciduous trees** lose their leaves every year. Most deciduous trees have thin, soft leaves that dry out easily. These are shed just before winter, when the temperature drops. If the ground freezes, there is less water available. If deciduous trees kept their leaves at this time, too much precious water would be lost through them.

Trees that do not shed their leaves all at once are known as **evergreen**. Unlike deciduous trees, they have tough, waxy leaves, which means they lose less water. They can survive and grow in places where little water is available. Keeping their leaves also means that they can continue to make food during the winter, even though there is less sunlight available.

EPHEMERALS

Plants with very short life cycles are called **ephemeral plants**. They are often found where the right growth conditions occur for a limited time, such as in deserts. The plants grow quickly from seeds which have been inactive in the ground. They bloom and produce seeds, which may also then grow, bloom and produce seeds, and so on, until conditions become unsuitable again.

Leaves on deciduous trees change colour before they fall. New leaves grow in spring, when the temperature rises.

Conifers such as these have narrow, waxy leaves with a small surface area. Little water is lost through them.

During the brief rainy season, these desert plants have bloomed, creating a carpet of flowers.

In some places, such as grasslands, there are two seasons: rainy and dry. The trees there shed their leaves at the beginning of the dry season, when the moisture level of the soil drops below a certain point. The leaves begin to grow back at the start of the rainy season, when water is available again.

See for yourself

Next time you are in a wooded area, look closely at the trees. See if you can find examples of both deciduous and evergreen trees, and compare the leaves. Deciduous leaves are flat, with thin veins running through them. Evergreen leaves tend to be waxy and pointed.

Internet links

• Go to www.usborne-quicklinks.com for a link to the **BrainPop Web site** to watch a movie about autumn leaves.

• Go to www.usborne-quicklinks.com for a link to the **Desert Museum Web site** to explore images and information about desert plants.

• Go to www.usborne-quicklinks.com for a link to the **California Forestry Association Web site**. Learn about the life cycle of trees by clicking on "About Forests" then "The Forest Cycle".

• Go to www.usborne-quicklinks.com for a link to the **Better Homes and Gardens Web site** to use an online plant encyclopedia.

PLANTS AND PEOPLE

The world can be divided into **biomes**. Each is a region with a unique climate and type of soil. A biome supports **ecosystems** – groups of plants and animals which interact with each other and their surroundings. Many ecosystems are damaged by the way people use the land.

Map showing main world biomes

Key to biomes

☐ Tropical rainforest
☐ Deciduous forest
☐ Mountains
☐ Coniferous forest
☐ Scrubland
☐ Temperate grassland
☐ Tundra
☐ Tropical grassland
☐ Desert
☐ Polar areas (little plant life)

Tropical rainforests contain a huge number of plants, which grow in layers. Treetops form the highest layer, and ground plants form the lowest. Each layer supports different forms of life.

Orchid

Deciduous forests generally grow in layers. At the top are tall deciduous trees*. Beneath is a layer of small trees and saplings, then a layer of shrubs. Next, there are a number of smaller plants, and finally a layer of mosses and lichens on the ground.

Oak leaf

Mountains are cold and bleak. Only low-growing plants such as mosses and shrubs grow on them.

Coniferous forests contain large numbers of conifers. They are usually found in areas where the soil is frozen for part of the year. This makes it difficult for plants to obtain water. Conifers have narrow, tough leaves called **needles** which reduce water loss.

Silver fir cone

Scrublands mainly contain shrubs. Many of these have small, leathery or needle-like leaves, which help to prevent water loss in the dry season.

Temperate grasslands (also known as **prairies** or **steppes**) contain many different types of grasses, but few trees. Their rich mixture of grasses is food for many different grazing animals.

Tundra regions are cold and windy. They contain low-growing plants, such as lichens, mosses and small shrubs. The temperature is too low for large plants such as trees.

Lichen

Tropical grasslands have a permanent cover of grasses, and sometimes also trees and shrubs. During the long dry season, there are many fires. These leave behind ashes which help to fertilize the soil.

Big bluestem grass

Deserts are hot and dry. Desert plants generally have a thick, waxy outer covering and slim leaves, to reduce water loss.

By clearing large areas such as this for farmland, there is a danger that we are losing too many natural habitats, including hedgerows and woodland.

* Deciduous trees, 47.

FOOD FOR ALL

For thousands of years, people have found ways of producing the food they need from the land around them. But as the human population grows, more and more food is needed. This means using more space to grow crops, or using existing farmland more efficiently. Some farming methods have a disastrous effect on ecosystems, though.

Here, a huge area of land has been cleared for growing crops, destroying the ecosystem which was there before.

Since farming began, people have identified plants with useful features, such as bigger fruit or better resistance to pests, and have used their seeds to grow better crops. This is called **selective breeding**. Overuse of selective breeding may lead to a loss of **biodiversity** – the huge variety of living things on Earth.

Intensive farming uses chemical fertilizers, pesticides, machinery and other methods to grow the most crops possible. But these methods return very few natural substances to the soil, and the chemicals can harm the land and animals living on it.

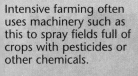

Intensive farming often uses machinery such as this to spray fields full of crops with pesticides or other chemicals.

GENETIC MODIFICATION

A living thing's characteristics are controlled by genes* in its cells. These are inherited from parents through reproduction, so cannot be passed naturally from one type of living thing to a different type.

Scientists, though, are able to take a gene for a certain useful feature from one organism and place it in another of a different kind. This is called **genetic modification**. Food produced like this is known as **GM food**.

It is possible, for instance, to take a gene which makes a fish resistant to the cold, and place it in a tomato plant. This creates tomato plants which can survive in cold weather.

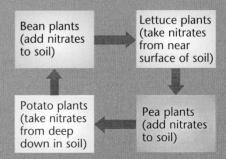

These GM tomatoes look like ordinary tomatoes. Many people who want to avoid buying GM food think it should be clearly labelled.

Some people think that GM crops could help to solve the problem of food shortages around the world. Others believe that adding genetically altered organisms to the natural world could cause irreversible damage to the environment.

Until more is known about its long-term effects, it is hard to know how helpful or harmful genetic modification will be.

ORGANIC FARMING

Organic farming works closely with nature by not adding artificial chemicals to the soil. For instance, instead of using chemical pesticides, some organic farmers plant onions among their crops. The strong smell of onions masks the smell of the crops, and pests are not attracted.

Organic farmers often use a method called **crop rotation**. Crops which use or replace certain minerals, such as nitrates, are planted in different fields each year. Manure and compost are used as fertilizers to help the crops to grow. This method keeps levels of natural substances balanced in the soil.

Example of crop rotation

Bean plants (add nitrates to soil) → Lettuce plants (take nitrates from near surface of soil) → Pea plants (add nitrates to soil) → Potato plants (take nitrates from deep down in soil) → Bean plants

Some people prefer to eat organically grown food because they know it is entirely natural and free from harmful chemicals.

Internet links

• Go to www.usborne-quicklinks.com for a link to the **Evergreen Project Web site** for information on world biomes.

• Go to www.usborne-quicklinks.com for a link to the **Smithsonian Institute Web site** for "Seeds of Change" gardens.

• Go to www.usborne-quicklinks.com for a link to the **Friends of the Earth Web site** for the potential dangers of GM foods.

• Go to www.usborne-quicklinks.com for a link to the **Monsanto Web site** for the potential benefits of GM foods.

• Go to www.usborne-quicklinks.com for a link to the **Farm School Web site** for an interactive look at family farming.

* Genes, 54-55.

NATURAL CYCLES

Plants and animals need carbon, nitrogen, oxygen and water to keep them alive. These vital substances are constantly recycled between the air, land and living things, which means that plants and animals need never run out of them. However, natural cycles are easily disturbed, especially by some human activities that release harmful substances into the environment.

Some fungi break down dead matter. This returns vital chemicals to the soil.

THE NITROGEN CYCLE

All living things need **nitrogen** to make essential chemicals called **proteins**. Before plants and animals can use nitrogen, it must be combined with oxygen to form **nitrates**. Lightning forms some nitrates from nitrogen in the air. Certain types of bacteria also form nitrates. They mostly live inside the roots of vegetables called legumes, for example peas and beans.

When a plant or animal dies, fungi and bacteria break it down. This releases nitrogen into the soil as a chemical called **ammonia**. **Nitrogen-fixing bacteria** in the soil change the ammonia into nitrates, which are taken in by plants. Animals gain these nitrates by eating plants, or animals that have eaten plants.

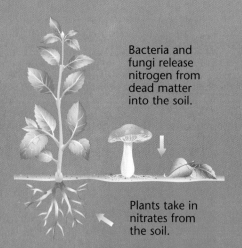

Bacteria and fungi release nitrogen from dead matter into the soil.

Plants take in nitrates from the soil.

THE CARBON CYCLE

All living things need **carbon** to live and grow. Plants obtain it from carbon dioxide in the air. During photosynthesis*, they use carbon dioxide to make food substances called **carbohydrates**.

Plants take in carbon dioxide during the day to help them make food.

At night, they give out carbon dioxide when food is not being produced.

Inside living things, internal respiration* turns carbohydrates into energy, producing carbon dioxide as waste. Carbon dioxide is also released into the atmosphere when organic matter is burned or broken down in the soil.

THE WATER CYCLE

Water is constantly recycled through the air, rivers and seas. Water that falls as rain drains int rivers, then into the sea. It turns to vapour, forming tiny droplets in the air. These form clouds, an water falls back to Earth as rain.

Plants transpire (release water vapour) through their leaves. Most animals also release water when they breathe out.

Water vapour is released through the surface of the leaves.

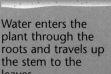

Water enters the plant through the roots and travels up the stem to the leaves.

See for yourself

Plants that grow in towns may be harmed by particles of dirt from traffic exhaust. On a dry day, gather a few leaves from trees or bushes growing in a town where there is lots of traffic passing through.

Next, take a damp cloth, and rub the upper surface of the leaves. You may find that a layer of dirt from the polluted air rubs off. This blocks out light that the leaves need to make food for the plant, making it less healthy.

Internal respiration, 23; Photosynthesis, 22.

UPSET BALANCE

People can upset the balance of natural cycles in various ways. For example, in some parts of the world, forests are burned down to make way for farming or building. Burning releases carbon, which forms carbon dioxide in the air.

The remaining plants do not remove this carbon dioxide fast enough during the process of photosynthesis*, so it builds up in the atmosphere.

The dense layer of carbon dioxide traps the Sun's heat around the Earth, creating what is known as the **greenhouse effect**. This is believed to cause **global warming**, a dangerous increase in the Earth's overall temperature.

Here, a large area of forest is being burned to make way for building and farming. Burning such as this increases the level of carbon dioxide in the atmosphere.

Pollution can also affect the growth patterns of living things. **Lichens** are simple living things made up of a fungus and an alga growing together. In areas with little or no pollution, shrubby lichens may be seen growing on trees. In very polluted areas, there are large amounts of green algae, but no lichens.

Green algae grow on trees in very polluted areas.

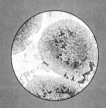
Leafy lichens grow on walls. They are found in areas with some pollution.

Shrubby lichens grow on trees in cleaner areas.

PLANTS UNDER THREAT

Some plants are directly threatened by human activities. For instance, golden barrel cacti are now very rare in Mexico, because they have been collected illegally and sold.

Golden barrel cactus
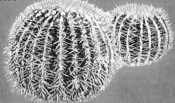

In Wales, seeds from the last tufted saxifrage plants in the country were grown into new plants. These were replanted in the wild to try to save the species from dying out. This was successful, but global warming is once again threatening the cold mountain areas in which they live.

Tufted saxifrage

Internet links

• Go to **www.usborne-quicklinks.com** for a link to the **Alien Explorer Web site** for clear, concise explanations of the carbon, nitrogen and water cycles.

• Go to **www.usborne-quicklinks.com** for links to the **Beakman & Jax Web site** to find activities related to global warming, acid rain and the ozone layer.

• Go to **www.usborne-quicklinks.com** for a link to the **Biocontrol 4 Kids Web site** to learn why plants are so important.

• Go to **www.usborne-quicklinks.com** for a link to the **How Stuff Works Web site** to discover the nutrients plants need.

• Go to **www.usborne-quicklinks.com** for a link to the **Shades of Green Web site** where you can find out how forests are put in danger.

Photosynthesis, 22.

CLASSIFYING PLANTS

In order to make living things easier to study, scientists organize them into groups with similar features. This process is called **classification**. Plants are usually classified by comparing the structure of their stems and leaves, as well as the arrangement and types of their reproductive parts.

THE KINGDOMS OF LIFE

The largest groups into which scientists divide living things are called **kingdoms**. There are five main kingdoms:

Monera

Bacteria

Simple microscopic organisms, such as bacteria, which do not have a nucleus* in their cells.

Protista

Amoeba

Single-celled organisms, such as amoebas, which share features with both plants and animals.

Plants

Living things such as trees and grass, which contain chlorophyll*. Most make their own food by photosynthesis*, but a small number digest other living things.

Yellow stargrass flowers

Fungi

Plant-like organisms that lack chlorophyll, and therefore cannot photosynthesize. Some break down dead matter, while others feed on living things.

Entoloma fungus

Animals

Creatures that can usually move around, and eat plants or other animals for food. Mammals and insects are examples of animals.

Pika

IDENTIFICATION

Scientists classify living things by identifying their main features and comparing them with those of similar species. One method used to compare features is called a **biological key**. A key is typically arranged in stages, with a choice of features at every stage. Each choice leads to another, until the organism is identified.

A key with two choices at each stage is called a **dichotomous key**. You can use the dichotomous key on the right to identify the six leaves above it. Pick one statement from each pair that describes the leaf you want to identify.

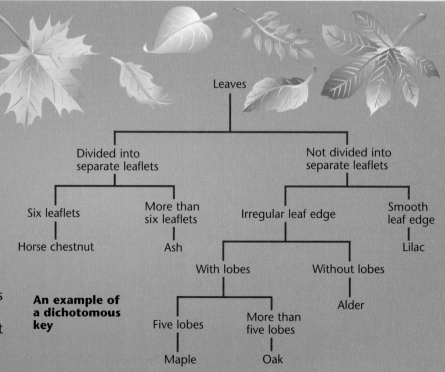

An example of a dichotomous key

* Chlorophyll, 8, 22; Nucleus, 8; Photosynthesis, 22.

THE PLANT KINGDOM

Plants are arranged in large groups called **divisions**. The plant kingdom has two main divisions: plants which contain fluid-carrying vascular tissue, and plants which do not. These divisions then break down into further, smaller categories, based mainly on the plant's reproductive structures.

VASCULAR PLANTS

Vascular plants are divided into two categories: those which produce seeds, and those which do not. Plants which produce seeds can be divided into two further groups, the gymnosperms and the angiosperms.

In **gymnosperms**, the seeds are not contained within a fruit. There are four types of gymnosperms.

Conifers are usually tree-sized plants, with waxy needle-like or scaly leaves. They produce cones, which contain their seeds.

Larch cone

Cycads produce very large cones. These grow in the middle of a circle of spiky leaves.

Cycad cone

Ginkgoes are direct relatives of ancient seed-carrying plants. They produce fleshy cones and have soft, fan-shaped leaves.

Ginkgo leaf

Gnetae are a small group of plants that grow in very hot areas. They mostly have tough, leathery leaves.

Welwitschia

Angiosperms is the name given to the many thousands of different flowering plants. They all produce seeds which are enclosed within a fruit of some kind. Flowering plants can be divided into two further groups: monocotyledons and dicotyledons.

Monocotyledons have one cotyledon (simple first leaf). Their vascular bundles are scattered throughout the stem.

Hosta

Dicotyledons have two cotyledons. Their vascular bundles are arranged in a regular pattern inside the stem (see page 13).

Lesser celandine

Seedless vascular plants have a simple structure, and do not produce flowers. They reproduce using spores*.

Horsetails produce spores inside cones. Their leaves are arranged in rings around the stem.

Horsetail

Ferns reproduce either by producing rhizomes*, or by making spores. These are produced on the underside of the fern's leafy fronds.

Bracken

Club mosses are related to ferns. Their spores are carried in tight, club-shaped spirals at the end of their stalks.

Stag's horn club moss

NON-VASCULAR PLANTS

Plants without vascular tissue, such as mosses and liverworts, are known as **bryophytes**. They are usually small, with single-celled root-like structures, and simple leaves. They have no flowers and therefore reproduce using spores. Most live in damp, shady places.

Mosses on a rock

Liverwort

Summary of divisions in the plant kingdom

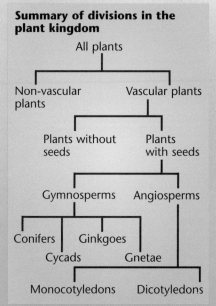

Internet links

• Go to **www.usborne-quicklinks.com** for a link to the **Natural Perspective Web site** for a good description of classification and divisions in the plant kingdom.

• Go to **www.usborne-quicklinks.com** for a link to the **Online Biology Book Web site** to take an in-depth look at all the main divisions of the plant kingdom.

• Go to **www.usborne-quicklinks.com** for a link to the **Gingko Web pages** for lots of information about gingkoes.

* Rhizomes, 36; Spores, 41.

53

GENETICS

Genetics is the branch of biology which studies how different characteristics are passed from one generation to the next. This process is known as **heredity**. An Austrian monk named Gregor Mendel was the first to study heredity successfully, using pea plants. He used the term "particles" to describe the inherited information which determines various features, but we know them now as genes.

Gregor Mendel (1822-84). His studies formed the basis of modern genetics.

BASIC GENETICS

Features (or **traits**) are passed from parents to offspring in structures called **chromosomes**. These are found in the cells of every living thing. A chromosome contains a single molecule of **DNA** (**deoxyribonucleic acid**), which is made up of a long chain of chemicals called **genes**. These contain coded information about all the organism's traits.

INHERITANCE

A plant or animal inherits two genes, one from each parent, which control any given trait. Mendel studied this effect using pea plants which produced either smooth seeds or wrinkled seeds. He saw that if a "wrinkled" plant was bred with a "smooth" plant, the offspring would have smooth seeds. This meant the "wrinkled" trait was being **masked** in that generation. It could reappear in the next generation, though.

Masking takes place when one gene, known as the **dominant** gene, overrides the instructions on the other, called the **recessive** gene. Recessive traits are only seen when two recessive genes are paired together.

INCOMPLETE DOMINANCE

If neither gene in a pair is dominant, it produces an effect called **incomplete dominance** or **blending**. For example, if a white flower were bred with a red flower, and neither colour was dominant, the offspring would be pink – a mixture of the two shades.

LABELLING TRAITS

The standard method of labelling genes in an organism uses two letters. Capital letters represent dominant traits, small letters represent recessive traits. For instance:

AA represents a plant with two dominant genes. It produces smooth seeds.
aa represents a plant with two recessive genes. It produces wrinkled seeds.

Aa or **aA** represents a plant with one of both kinds of gene. The "smooth" gene masks the "wrinkled" gene, so the plant produces smooth seeds.

Gene combinations

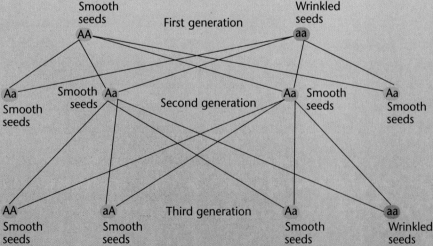

The diagram above shows all possible gene combinations in each generation of pea plant. Lines indicate which parent a gene came from. The "wrinkled" trait is masked in all second generation plants (with Aa or aA genes). It can reappear in the third generation when some of the offspring receive an "a" gene from both parents.

GENETICS IN ACTION

The understanding of genetics gained from Mendel's work and later studies led to the creation of many new areas of biology. Scientists now know how to make genetically identical clones of plants and animals, transplant genes from one living thing to another, and much more. These techniques have many uses, from studying inherited diseases to growing healthier, stronger crops. Below, you can read about the main types of gene technology.

SELECTIVE BREEDING

The earliest form of genetics was **selective breeding**, also known as **artificial selection**. This involves carefully breeding together individuals which carry desirable traits, so that the traits are passed on. Using plants or animals of the same variety is called **pure-breeding**. Using different varieties is called **cross-breeding**.

GENETIC ENGINEERING

Genetic engineering is used to produce animals and plants with a particular trait, (normally one which would not occur naturally in that species) by altering their genes in some way. This usually involves introducing a gene from another, unrelated species.

A plant or animal which has had a trait introduced from another species is described as **transgenic**. This technique can be used in animal herds and food crops, to give useful characteristics such as hardiness or improved flavour. Food produced in this way is commonly known as **GM (genetically modified)** food. For more about GM food, see page 49.

HELP OR HARM?

Introducing traits from outside the species can have lots of benefits to a plant, such as increased resistance to pests, cold and other hazards. It is not yet understood, though, what effects transgenes may have on the environment. For instance, if genetically modified plants were to reproduce with ordinary ones, the transgene would be very difficult to remove. It might prove harmful to animals which consume the plant, and the animals which in turn consume them.

CLONING

Unlike animals, many varieties of fully-grown adult plants can be regrown from single, modified cells called protoplasts. The new plant created by this process, called a **clone**, is genetically identical to the original plant. You can learn about another type of cloning, called vegetative reproduction, on pages 36-37.

Cloning has been very useful in studying the effects of genetic modification. Researchers can alter the genetic information in a cell, let the cell develop into a fully-grown plant, then examine the effects of the genetic alteration, within a relatively short period of time. Doing the same thing with animal cells is much more difficult and time-consuming.

Roses do not have a gene for blue colouring, so this rose was made blue using dyes. The only way to make a real blue rose is to add a "blue" gene from a different type of blue flower.

Internet links

• Go to **www.usborne-quicklinks.com** for links to a **Johann Gregor Mendel biography** and the **Reflections on Gregor Mendel Web sites**, both of which offer good introductions to the life and work of Mendel.

• Go to **www.usborne-quicklinks.com** for a link to the **Introduction to Genetics Web site** for an excellent and very thorough introduction to genetics.

• Go to **www.usborne-quicklinks.com** for a link to the **Pea Soup - Pea Experiment Web site**, where you can learn more about genetics by growing your own virtual pea plants.

USEFUL PLANTS AND FUNGI

On this page, you will find details of a number of plants and fungi which are used by people for medicine, food and other purposes. The type of plant used for a particular purpose varies greatly around the world; for instance, in one country a fruit might be eaten simply for its taste, but in another it may be used for its medicinal qualities. The uses given here are the most common in the developed world.

Common name	Latin name	Common use
Aloe vera	Aloe vera	Used as a natural medicine; speeds up rate of wound healing
Aniseed	Pimpinella anisum	Used to flavour foods and, traditionally, to aid digestion
Belladonna	Atropa belladonna	Contains a chemical used to dilate (widen) the pupils during eye examinations
Camomile	Anthemis nobilis	Flower extract can be used internally as an antidepressant and painkiller, and externally to soothe skin
Coffee	Coffea arabica	Beans produced by this plant are ground to make coffee
Corn	Zea mays	Food crop; also used as animal feed and a source of ethanol, starch and sweeteners
Cotton	Gossypium hirsutum	Used to make clothing and materials
Cocoa palm	Theobroma cacao	Beans from the cocoa palm are used to make chocolate
Dandelion	Taraxacum officinale	Herbal remedy, used to aid function of the liver and kidneys. Can also be used to flavour drinks
Eucalyptus	Eucalyptus globulus	Used to treat colds and sore throats
Foxglove	Digitalis purpurea	Digitalin, a chemical found in foxgloves, is used as a major treatment for heart disease
Garlic	Allium sativum	Used in cooking and as a natural health supplement, especially to treat blood-related disorders
Grape	Vitis species	Many varieties. Can be eaten raw, or crushed and fermented to make wine
Lemon	Citrus limon	Used to make flavourings and drinks. Also used in cold remedies, because of high vitamin C content
Marigold	Calendula officinalis	Marigold oil is used to treat skin disorders
Olive	Olea europaea	Source of olive oil, widely used in cooking
Penicillium	Penicillium notatum	A fungus used to make penicillin, an important antibiotic
Peppermint	Mentha piperita	Used as a food flavouring and as a medicine to settle the digestive system
Potato	Solanum tuberosum	Major food crop
Rice	Oryza sativa	Major food crop
Rosy periwinkle	Vinca rosea	This flower is the source of vincristine and vinblastine, two major drugs used to treat leukemia in children
Soy bean	Glycine max	Food crop
Spruce	Picea species	Pulp of this and other softwood trees, e.g. firs, is commonly used to make paper fibre
St John's Wort	Hypericum perforatum	Used as a natural antidepressant and pain reliever
Sugar maple	Acer saccharum	Sap of this tree is used to make maple syrup
Tea plant	Thea bohea	Leaves are used to make tea
Tobacco plant	Nicotiana tabacum	Leaves of this plant are cured (dried) to provide tobacco for cigarettes and related products
Tomato	Lycopersicon esculentum	Food crop
Wheat	Triticum sativum	Food crop, used to make flour
Witch Hazel	Hamamelis virginiana	A shrub, used to reduce pain and swelling of bruises
Yeast	Saccharomyces cerevisiae	A fungus, used to make bread and alcoholic drinks

TEST YOURSELF

1. Which of the following is found in plant cells but not animal cells?
A. a cell wall
B. a nucleus
C. cytoplasm *(Page 8)*

2. A carrot is
A. an aerial root
B. an adventitious root
C. a tap root *(Page 11)*

3. Water is taken into a plant through
A. its flowers
B. the root hairs in the soil
C. the surface of its leaves *(Page 11)*

4. The tissue in plants which carries water upwards is
A. xylem
B. phloem
C. cambium *(Page 12)*

5. In an older plant, xylem and phloem join up to form
A. lenticels
B. vascular bundles
C. a vascular cylinder *(Pages 14-15)*

6. Which tree has compound leaves?
A. horse chestnut
B. lime
C. oak *(Pages 16-17)*

7. Leaf stomata are found mainly on
A. both upper and lower surfaces
B. the lower surface
C. the upper surface *(Page 18)*

8. Water loss from the leaves through the stomata is called
A. transpiration
B. translocation
C. respiration *(Page 20)*

9. Chlorophyll is vital to plants because
A. it absorbs energy from the Sun
B. it provides food
C. it colours it green *(Page 22)*

10. Photosynthesis can be expressed as
A. water + oxygen + energy → carbohydrates + carbon dioxide
B. oxygen + carbon dioxide + water → carbohydrates + energy
C. carbon dioxide + water + energy → carbohydrates + oxygen *(Page 22)*

11. Plants respire
A. when photosynthesis stops
B. only at night
C. all the time *(Page 23)*

12. A plant which feeds on dead matter is
A. a parasite
B. a saprotroph
C. an epiphyte *(Page 24)*

13. Which is a carnivorous plant?
A. mistletoe
B. strangler fig
C. sundew *(Pages 24-25)*

14. Male reproductive cells of a plant are called
A. anthers
B. pollen
C. pollen sacs *(Page 29)*

15. Female reproductive cells of a plant are called
A. ovaries
B. carpels
C. ovules *(Page 29)*

16. Pollination occurs when
A. a pollen grain connects with an ovule by a pollen tube
B. a pollen grain forms a pollen tube
C. a pollen grain lands on the stigma of another plant *(Page 30)*

17. Which statement is true? Most wind-pollinated plants
A. produce large quantities of smooth, light pollen grains
B. have large sepals and petals
C. have brightly-coloured, sweet-scented flowers *(Page 31)*

18. Which of these is a true fruit?
A. strawberry
B. cherry
C. apple *(Page 32)*

19. Which plant has seeds dispersed by the wind?
A. sycamore
B. goosegrass
C. pea *(Page 34)*

20. In order to germinate, seeds need warmth, oxygen and
A. water
B. light
C. food *(Page 35)*

21. The first root produced by a seed is
A. the plumule
B. the hilum
C. the radicle *(Page 35)*

22. Long side shoots which run overground and can develop into new plants are called
A. tubers
B. rhizomes
C. runners *(Page 36)*

23. A plant adapted to life in fresh water is
A. a hydrophyte
B. a lithophyte
C. a halophyte *(Page 38)*

24. The rapid reproduction of plants in water with high nitrate levels is
A. intoxication
B. eutrophication
C. adaptation *(Page 39)*

25. Ferns, mosses and liverworts
A. can reproduce by making spores
B. produce large numbers of flowers
C. cannot grow in damp, shady places *(Pages 40-41)*

26. Penicillin is made from a type of
A. alga
B. fungus
C. liverwort *(Page 43)*

27. A plant which takes two years to complete its life cycle is called
A. a perennial
B. an annual
C. a biennial *(Page 46)*

28. Plants which lose all their leaves once a year are called
A. xerophytes
B. evergreen
C. deciduous *(Page 47)*

29. Prairies and steppes are forms of which biome?
A. tundra
B. temperate grassland
C. tropical grassland *(Page 48)*

30. Plants take in nitrogen from their surroundings in the form of
A. ammonia
B. nitrogen gas
C. nitrates *(Page 50)*

Answers

1.A 2.C 3.B 4.A 5.C 6.A 7.B 8.A 9.A 10.C 11.C 12.B 13.C 14.B 15.C 16.A 17.A 18.B 19.A 20.A 21.C 22.C 23.A 24.B 25.A 26.B 27.C 28.C 29.B 30.C

57

A-Z OF SCIENTIFIC TERMS

Abscission layer A layer that forms at the base of a dead leaf's stalk, cutting it off from the body of the plant before it falls off, and showing as a **leaf scar** once the leaf has fallen.

achene A small, dry fruit with one seed.

adventitious roots Roots that grow directly from a bulb or gardener's stem cutting.

aerial roots Roots that do not usually grow in the ground. They absorb moisture from the air.

aggregate (or **compound**) **fruit** Fruit, such as raspberries, which are made up of fleshy beads called **drupelets**, each with one seed.

algae A large, varied group of simple water plants, ranging from single-celled diatoms to large seaweeds.

alternation of generations A process in many flowerless plants, where one generation reproduces sexually and the next asexually.

annual ring A single ring of xylem in a cross section of an older plant, showing one year's growth.

annuals Plants that live and die in one year.

anther A pod-like structure at the end of a stamen which contains pollen sacs.

angiosperms Flowering plants. Their seeds are contained within some kind of fruit. There are two types: monocotyledons and dicotyledons.

apical meristems The main areas of growth on a plant, at the tips of the shoot and root (see also *meristem*).

artificial propagation The creation of new plants for gardening or commercial reasons by making use of their ability to reproduce vegetatively (growing them from cuttings, bulbs etc).

artificial selection Breeding together individual living things with desired traits (see *heredity*), so that these traits appear in the new individuals.

asexual reproduction The creation of a new organism from a single parent.

autotrophic A term describing plants that make their own food by photosynthesis.

auxins Growth hormones which control the responses of plants to stimuli such as light.

axil The place on a plant between a shoot or leaf stalk and the stem. A bud growing there is an **axillary bud** (or **lateral**, or **secondary**, **bud**).

Bacteria A varied group of microscopic organisms without cell nuclei.

biennials Plants that take two years to complete their life cycle.

biodiversity The huge variety of living things on Earth.

biological key A method of identifying the species of an organism by asking a series of questions about it, often shown as a tree diagram.

bipinnate leaf A pinnate leaf whose leaflets are also pinnate.

blending See *incomplete dominance*.

bract A leaf at the base of a flower stalk which often serves to protect the bud.

bryophytes Plants without vascular tissue, such as mosses and liverworts.

Cambium A narrow layer of thin-walled cells that produces new xylem and phloem.

capillary action The process by which a fluid is drawn up a narrow channel because of the attraction between its molecules and those of the channel.

carbohydrates Organic compounds containing carbon, hydrogen and oxygen. The simple carbohydrate glucose is produced from carbon dioxide and water by photosynthesis in plants, and is then either stored as starch, or used immediately in internal respiration to give energy for growth.

carbon cycle The process by which the element carbon from the atmosphere enters the food chain through photosynthesis and returns to the atmosphere through internal respiration and decay.

carotene A natural pigment which produces red or orange colours.

carpel (or **pistil**) The female reproductive organ of a plant. See also *stigma*; *style*; *ovary*.

caryopsis Another word for a grain.

cell membrane A thin layer between a plant cell's cytoplasm and the cell wall.

cell plate The dividing line that separates the cytoplasm during cytokinesis.

cell sap A sugary liquid found inside the vacuole in plant cells.

cellulose A tough, glucose-based substance, from which cell walls are made.

cell wall The tough outer layer of a plant cell.

chlorophyll A green pigment found in many plant cells. It absorbs light for photosynthesis.

chloroplasts Organelles in a plant cell which contain chlorophyll.

chromoplasts Organelles that contain pigment, and so give many plants their characteristic colours.

chromosomes Structures containing the chemical DNA (deoxyribonucleic acid) found in each cell nucleus of a plant or animal. Each chromosome is made up of smaller chemical units called genes, which together contain all the information needed to develop that individual plant or animal.

classification In biology, a method of sorting organisms into groups, which are themselves divided into smaller groups.

cloning Creating a new, genetically identical individual from an original one.

club mosses Low-growing flowerless plants, related to ferns. They have scaly leaves and produce spores inside club-shaped growths called strobili.

collenchyma A type of supporting ground tissue with long, thick-walled cells, found in cortex.

compensation points The two points in every 24 hours when the processes of photosynthesis and internal respiration in a plant are exactly balanced.

composite bulb A bulb made up of sections called **cloves**, each one able to produce an individual plant.

compound fruit See *aggregate fruit*.

compound leaf A leaf made up of more than one **leaflet** growing from a central stalk.

conifers Trees or bushes, all gymnosperms, with waxy needle-like or scaly leaves, which bear cones containing their seeds. Most are evergreen.

cork cambium See *phellogen*.

corm A short, thick plant stem base, swollen with food, from which a new shoot grows in the spring.

corolla All the petals of a flower.

cortex The ground tissue that surround vascular tissue in a vascular plant.

cotyledon (or **seed leaf**) A simple first leaf (not a true leaf) which forms in a seed, and only emerges above ground in some plants.

critical length A certain length of daytime, crucial to triggering the production of flowers by a flowering plant.

crop rotation A farming practice in which crops which use or replace certain minerals are planted in different fields each year.

cross-pollination Pollination in which pollen from one plant pollinates another plant of the same kind.

cuticle The protective, waterproof outer layer of the epidermis of a plant, made of a waxy substance called **cutin**.

cycads A group of gymnosperms which produce very large cones, each in the middle of a circle of spiky leaves.

cytokinesis The division of the cytoplasm after meiosis or mitosis.

cytoplasm The gel-like substance inside a cell in which organelles are suspended.

Deciduous trees Trees that shed their leaves in the autumn.

decussate leaves Pairs of opposite leaves, each growing from a stem at right angles to the pair before.

dermal Of or relating to the surface layer of a plant.

desmids Types of single-celled freshwater algae.

diatoms Types of mostly single-celled algae with hard, glassy body cases.

dichotomous key A biological key in which there are only two choices at each stage.

dicotyledon A plant, such as a pea, that has two cotyledons.

dioecious A term describing plant species in which individuals have either staminate (male) or pistillate (female) flowers.

dispersal The scattering of seeds away from the parent plant.

dominant gene See *masking*.

drupe A succulent fruit, such as a plum, with a single hard-cased seed in the middle.

drupelets See *aggregate fruit*.

dry fruit dry cases that hold seeds until they are ripe, for example a hazelnut.

Embryo A developing organism. A plant embryo develops inside a seed.

emergent plants Plants which thrive in wet or water-covered ground. Their leaves and stems are mostly visible above the water.

endodermis The innermost layer of the cortex.

endosperm A tissue layer in a seed that surrounds and feeds the growing plant.

enzyme A chemical substance that aids and speeds up the internal processes of living things.

ephemeral The term used to describe organisms with very short life cycles, such as some desert flowers.

epidermis The thin outer layer of tissue on a young plant, replaced as the plant gets older by bark above ground, and by exodermis and then bark below ground.

epigeal germination The type of germination in which the cotyledons emerge above ground, below the first, true leaves.

epiphyte An organism which makes its own food, but grows high up on other plants to get a better share of the light and water.

eutrophication An overgrowth of plants in a body of water due to high levels of nitrates or phosphates and other compounds found in fertilizers.

exodermis An outer layer of hard cells on the root of an older plant, which replaces the epidermis and is replaced by bark.

False fruit Fruit, such as strawberries, which develop from the receptacle and the ovary.

fertilization The joining of male and female sex cells to form the first cell of a new individual.

fibres Long, thin, supporting cells in the xylem of vascular plants.

fibrous roots A system of many equal-sized plant roots, all of which produce smaller roots.

filament The stalk of a stamen, which supports the anther.

florigen A growth hormone in plants that signals them to flower only when the nights are a certain length, different for each type of plant. See also *critical length*.

fronds The name given to the leaf-like structures of seaweeds and ferns.

fruiting body The part of a fungus where spores are produced.

fungi Plant-like organisms that cannot make their own food, and feed on dead or living plant and animal matter.

funicle The stalk which fixes an ovule to the inside wall of the ovary.

Gametes Male or female sex cells.

gametophyte A term describing a plant which produces male and female gametes. It grows as the sexual stage during alternation of generations.

gemmae Buds which form on a parent and develop into new plants. Forming buds in this way, called **gemmation**, is a type of asexual reproduction.

genes The pairs of chemical instructions (each one part of a chromosome) which together give all the information needed to build a living thing. See also *heredity*.

genetic engineering Altering an organism's genes in some way, so as to produce a desired result.

genetic modification A specific type of genetic engineering. It involves changing an organism by adding to it the specific gene for a desired feature from another organism. Food produced in this way is called **GM (genetically modified) food**, and the changed organism is described as **transgenic**.

geotropism The response of roots to gravity, by which they tend to grow downwards into the soil, towards minerals and water.

germination The point in a seed's growth into a seedling when the plumule and radicle break out of the seed case. See also *hypogeal, epigeal germination*.

ginkgo An ancient gymnosperm species with soft, fan-shaped leaves and fleshy cones.

glucose The simple carbohydrate produced by photosynthesis, and broken down during internal respiration to release energy.

gnetae A small group of gymnosperms with tough, leathery leaves, that grow in hot areas.

ground tissue Plant tissue that packs out and forms the bulk of young stems and roots.

guard cells A pair of crescent-shaped cells that open and close to control the amount of air and water entering or leaving a stoma.

guttation Water loss, in liquid form, through tiny holes in leaf tips and edges.

gymnosperms Vascular plants in which the seeds are not contained in a fruit.

Halophytes Plants that are specially adapted to live in salty areas.

haptotropism (or **thigmotropism**) The response of a plant to touch.

haustoria Thread-like structures used by some parasitic plants to attach themselves to a host.

hemiparasite A plant which takes water and minerals from other plants, but can also photosynthesize.

herbaceous A term describing plants with non-woody green stems.

heredity The passing on of characteristics, or **traits**, from one generation to the next, through genes. A gene for each trait is passed to an offspring from each parent.

hermaphrodite An organism that has both male and female sex cells.

hilum The mark on a seed which shows where the ovule was joined to the ovary.

holdfasts The root-like structures of seaweeds, which anchor them to objects such as rocks.

horsetails Vascular plants which produce spores in cones.

hydrophytes Plants adapted for life in fresh water.

hydrotropism The response of roots to water, by which they grow towards it.

hypogeal germination The type of germination in which the cotyledons remain below ground, inside the testa.

hyphae Thread-like structures forming the mycelium of a fungus. They absorb food from organic matter in the soil.

Incomplete dominance (or **blending**) A situation where neither of a pair of genes masks the other (see *masking*), and the result is a mixture of their instructions, for instance when genes for two different colours of flower produce a third, blended colour.

internal respiration The process by which living things use oxygen to break down their food, producing energy and releasing carbon dioxide.

internode The area of a plant stem or shoot between two nodes.

Key fruit See *samara*.

Lamina A simple leaf blade.
lateral bud See *axil*.
lateral root (or **secondary root**) A smaller root that grows from a plant's main root or roots.
leaf trace An area of vascular tissue which branches off that of a stem to become a leaf's central vein.
legume (or **pod**) A dry fruit with seeds attached to its inner wall, for example, a pea pod. A plant which produces legumes is described as **leguminous**.
lenticels Tiny openings in a tree's bark through which oxygen and carbon dioxide are exchanged.
lichen An organism made up of an alga and a fungus living in a symbiotic relationship.
lithophytes Plants which live on the surface of rocks.
liverworts Low-growing plants without true roots, stems or leaves, that grow in damp, shady places.

Masking The process by which one of the paired genes which determine a trait (see *heredity*) is "stronger", or **dominant**.
For instance, a plant with a gene for producing wrinkled seeds and a gene for producing smooth seeds will produce smooth seeds because that dominant gene masks the "weaker", **recessive** gene.
meiosis The division of the nucleus when a specialized plant cell divides to produce sex cells. The two new cells each have only half the original number of chromosomes, ready for when they join with another sex cell.
meristem An area of cells in a plant which divide to provide new growth.
mesophyll The interior tissue of a leaf, made up of the palisade and spongy layers, which surrounds the veins.
micropropagation A method of cloning a plant from cells taken from a growth area.
micropyle See *pollination*.
midrib The central vein of a leaf.
mildews Types of simple fungi, often seen as powdery black or white patches.
minerals Simple chemicals found in the soil which are essential to the proper development of a plant.
mitosis The division of the nucleus when a plant cell divides for growth or repair. The two new nuclei each contain the same number of chromosomes as the original nucleus.
Monera A kingdom of microscopic organisms, such as bacteria, which have no nuclei in their cells.
monocotyledon A plant, such as a grass, that has only one cotyledon.

monoecious A term describing a plant which has separate staminate and pistillate flowers.
moulds Types of simple fungi which form a furry growth on living or once-living matter.
mycelium The main, underground part of most fungi, made up of a mass of hyphae.
mycorrhizae Fungi which feed on the roots of living plants.

Natural selection The process whereby individuals with features which are best suited to their environment are more likely to survive and produce young. The young then inherit the parents' favourable features.
nectar A sweet, sticky substance produced by plants to attract pollinating insects.
nectary An area of cells at the base of a petal which produces nectar.
nitrates A group of naturally-occurring salts that are essential to plant growth.
nitrogen cycle The natural process by which nitrogen gas is converted into nitrates in the soil, used by plants, and returned again to the air.
nitrogen-fixing bacteria Bacteria which convert nitrogen gas into nitrogen compounds.
node The place on a plant stem where a leaf, or leaf stalk, has grown.
nucleus The part of a cell that controls all of its processes.

Organelle Any of the small parts in the cytoplasm of a cell. Different types of organelle have different functions.
ovary The female reproductive body which, in plants, contains ovules.
ovules The female sex cells of a plant, which develop into seeds after fertilization.

Palisade cells Column-shaped cells, containing many chloroplasts. They form the **palisade layer** on a leaf's upper side, beneath the epidermis.
palmate leaf A compound leaf with five or more leaflets growing from a single point.
parasite An organism which lives and feeds upon another (the host). It may cause harm to its host.
parenchyma A type of ground tissue with large cells and many air spaces, found in cortex.
perennials Plants that live for many years.
perfoliate leaves Single or paired leaves with their bases fused to a plant's stem.
petiole A leaf stalk.

phellogen (or **cork cambium**) A single layer of cells on the outside of a tree which constantly divide, building up the bark.
phloem The tissue in vascular plants which carries food, made in the leaves, to all the other parts of the plant.
photoperiodism A plant response by which it will only grow if light is available for a certain length of time (the **photoperiod**).
photosynthesis The process by which plants use energy from sunlight to power the production of food (glucose) from water and carbon dioxide.
phototropism The response of a plant in which it turns to face the light.
pinnate leaf A leaf in which the leaflets, called **pinnae**, are arranged in opposite pairs along the stalk.
pistil See *carpel*.
pistillate flower A flower which has only female reproductive parts.
plasmolysis A shrinking of protoplasm away from the cell wall due to extreme water loss.
plumule The part of a plant embryo which develops into the first shoot.
pod See *legume*.
pollen A plant's male reproductive cells.
pollination The process by which plants are fertilized. A pollen grain lands on the stigma and forms a **pollen tube**. This grows down into the ovary, entering the ovule through a tiny hole called a **micropyle**.
pome A false fruit, such as an apple, with a thick, fleshy outer layer and a core with seeds contained in a capsule.
primary root See *tap root*.
primary tissue The first tissue formed by a new plant.
prop roots A type of aerial root which grows outwards from the stem, then down into the ground. They are often found on plants which grow in ground that is under water.
protective adaptations Features developed through natural selection, which help to protect organisms from damage or danger.
proteins Natural substances containing nitrogen. They are produced in cells, and are essential for growth and tissue repair.
prothalli Flat, often heart-shaped gametophytes which grow from fern spores.
Protista A kingdom of single-celled organisms which combine features of both plants and animals.

Radicle The part of a plant embryo which develops into the plant's first root.
receptacle The expanded tip of a flower stalk, from which the bud grows.
recessive gene See *masking*.
reproduction The creation of new living things by existing ones.

rhizoids Short, hair-like organs that serve as roots in simple plants, such as liverworts.

rhizomes Stems which grow out horizontally underground, producing new buds and roots.

root pressure The water pressure in a plant's roots which pushes water up into the transpiration stream.

rosette (or **whorl**) A leaf arrangement in which a circle of leaves grows from one point.

runners (or **stolons**) Long side shoots put out by plants such as strawberries. New plants grow from points along them in a type of vegetative reproduction.

S aline Containing salt (sodium chloride).

samara (or **key fruit**) An achene with papery wings, such as a sycamore fruit.

saprotroph (or **saprophyte**) An organism such as a fungus, which does not make its own food, but lives off dead plant or animal matter.

secondary bud See *axil*.

secondary root See *lateral root*.

secondary thickening The process by which long-lived plants, such as trees, grow new tissue to support their original tissue.

seed leaf See *cotyledon*.

selective breeding The controlled breeding of organisms to produce individuals with desired features, such as hardiness.

self-pollination A type of pollination in which a plant pollinates itself.

sepals Leaf-like structures that provide a case to protect a bud.

serrate A term describing a leaf edge which has tiny jagged teeth.

sexual reproduction Reproduction which involves the joining of male and female sex cells.

shoot A new stem which grows out of a seed or off the main stem of a plant.

sieve plates Perforated ends of the cell walls between sieve tubes.

sieve tubes Fluid-carrying cells which make up the phloem of vascular plants.

sori Tiny sacs on the underside of fern fronds, where fern spores develop.

specialization The developed suitability of cells and organisms for a particular function, environment or way of life.

spongy cells Irregularly shaped cells which are spaced with air gaps. They make up the **spongy layer** beneath a leaf's palisade layer.

sporangia Tiny capsules, each on the end of a stalk, which grow on mosses, fungi and ferns. They contain spores.

spores 1. Reproductive cells produced by a sporophyte, which grow into new gametophytes. 2. Reproductive cells produced by fungi. They grow into new fungi as part of a repeated process of asexual reproduction.

sporophyte The spore-producing plant which is the asexual stage in the process of alternation of generations.

sporulation The production and release of spores.

stamens A plant's male reproductive organs.

staminate flower A flower which has only male reproductive parts.

starch The form in which glucose, produced by photosynthesis, is stored in plants.

stigma The sticky top part of a carpel, which traps pollen grains that touch it.

stipules A pair of small, stalkless leaves at the base of a leaf stalk, which protect the bud as it forms.

stolons See *runners*.

stomata Tiny holes on a leaf's underside, through which air and water move in and out.

strobili See *club mosses*.

style Part of the carpel which joins the stigma to the ovary.

submergent plants Plants, such as Canadian pondweed, in which most of the body grows underwater.

succulent fruit Fruit with thick, fleshy layers that are often tasty to eat.

symbiotic relationship A relationship between two organisms which benefits both (see also *lichen*).

T ap root (or **primary root**) A large plant root with smaller ones growing from it.

temperate Describes a climatic region with rainfall throughout the year and temperatures that vary with the seasons.

tendril A thread-like leaf or stem which twines around, or sticks to, a support.

terminal bud A bud which grows at the end of a plant stem or shoot.

ternate leaf A trifoliate leaf where each leaflet has three lobes.

testa A seed's tough, protective coat.

thallus The main body of a liverwort, held in the ground by rhizoids.

thigmotropism See *haptotropism*.

tissue Many cells of the same type grouped together.

tracheids Tubes that make up the xylem of non-flowering vascular plants.

transgenic See *genetic modification*.

translocation The movement of fluids inside a plant.

transpiration The loss of water, as vapour, through leaf stomata.

transpiration stream The upward movement of water in a plant, from the roots to the leaves.

trifoliate leaf A compound leaf with three leaflets growing from a single point.

tripinnate leaf A bipinnate leaf with a further branching of pinnate leaflets.

tropical Describes a climatic region between the tropics.

tropism The response of a plant to a stimulus. In **positive tropism**, a plant grows towards a stimulus; in **negative tropism** it grows away from it.

true fruit A fruit, such as the cherry, which develops from a plant's ovary.

tuber A swollen underground stem that stores food for a plant through the winter, such as that of the potato plant. New shoots grow from it in the spring.

tundra A region with harsh winds and low temperatures. Its underground soil is always frozen, so it has no trees.

turgor The state of a plant when its cell vacuoles are full of sap (**turgid**), making it stand firmly upright.

V acuole A fluid-filled sac inside a cell, filled with cell sap. Most plant cells have one large, permanent vacuole, containing cell sap.

variegated leaf A leaf patterned with two or more colours.

vascular A term describing something made up of, or containing, conducting vessels. In plants, it means having xylem and phloem.

vascular bundle One of the groups of xylem and phloem cells found in young stems.

vascular cylinder The ring of vascular tissue found in the stems of older dicotyledons, formed when the vascular bundles join up.

vegetative reproduction (or **vegetative propagation**) A type of asexual reproduction by which parts of plants grow into new plants.

vein A long strip of vascular tissue (xylem and phloem) in a leaf.

vessels Column-shaped cells with no dividing walls, which make up the xylem of flowering plants.

W horl See *rosette*.

wilting The drooping condition of a plant which is losing more water than it can take in.

woody plants Plants such as trees, whose stems and roots grow thicker each year. See also *secondary thickening*.

X anthophylls Pigments which produce yellow colours in plants.

xerophytes Plants such as cacti, which are specially adapted to live in very dry areas.

xylem The tissue in vascular plants which carries water and dissolved minerals, taken in by the roots, up to the leaves.

Y east A single-celled fungus used in brewing and bread-making.

Z one of elongation The area of new cells formed by dividing cells just behind a root tip.

zygote The first cell of a new organism, formed after fertilization.

INDEX

You will find the main explanations of indexed terms on the pages shown in bold type. It may be useful to look at the other pages for further information.

A

abscission layer **19**, 58
achenes **33**, 58
adventitious roots **11**, 58
aerial roots **11**, 58
aggregate fruit **32**, 58
air bladders **39**
algae **39**, 40, 51, 58
alternate leaves **17**
alternation of generations **41**, 58
ammonia **50**
amoeba **52**
angiosperms **28**, **53**, 58
animal pollination **30**
annual rings **15**, 58
annuals **46**, 58
anthers **29**, 58
apical meristems **10**, 58
artificial propagation **37**, 58
artificial selection **55**, 58
asexual reproduction **36-37**, 40-41, 58
autotrophic **22**, 58
auxins **26**, 58
axils **10**, 58
axillary buds **10**, 58 (axil)

B

bacteria 50, **52**, 58
bark 13, **15**
basal rosette **17**
berries **32**
biennials **46**, 58
biodiversity **49**, 58
biological keys **52**, 58
biomes **48**
bipinnate leaves **16**, 58
blending (See *incomplete dominance*)
bracts **17**, 58
bryophytes **53**, 58
buds **10**, 28
bulbs **11**, 36

C

cacti **44**, 51
cambium **12**, 14, 58
camouflage **45**
capillary action **20**, 58
carbohydrates **22**, **50**, 58
carbon **50**
    cycle 43, **50**, 58
    dioxide 22, 23, 50
carnivorous plants **25**, 27
carotene 19, 58

carpels **29**, 58
caryopsis **33**, 58
cells **8-9**, 18
cell
    division **9**, 12
    membranes **8**, 58
    plate **9**, 58
    repair 9
    sap **8**, 58
    walls **8**, 58
cellulose **8**, 58
cherries 32
chlorophyll **8**, 19, **22**, 42, 52, 58
chloroplasts **8**, 9, 18, **22**, 58
chromoplasts **8**, 58
chromosomes **54**, 58
chrysanthemum 27
classification **52-53**, 58
climate 48
clone (See *cloning*)
cloning **55**, 58
cloves **36**, 58 (composite bulb)
club mosses **40**, 53, 58
coastal plants **44**
collenchyma **13**, 58
compensation points **23**, 58
composite bulbs **36**, 58
compound
    fruit **32**, 58
    leaves **16**, 58
cones **33**
conifers 33, 47, 48, **53**, 58
coniferous forests **48**
cork cambium **15**, 58
corms **36**, 58
corolla **28**, 58
cortex **13**, 58
cotyledons **35**, 58
critical length **27**, 58
crop rotation **49**, 58
cross-breeding **55**
cross-pollination **30**, 58
cuticle **13**, 58
cutin **13**, 58 (cuticle)
cutting (plants) **37**
cyanobacteria 39
cycads **53**, 58
cytokinesis **9**, 59
cytoplasm **8**, 9, 12, 21, **59**

D

day-neutral plants **27**
deciduous
    forests **48**
    trees **47**, 48, 59
decussate leaves **17**, 59
dermal **59**
    tissue **9**, 13
desert plants **44**, 47
deserts 47, **48**
desmids **39**, 59
diatoms **39**, 59
dichotomous keys **52**, 59
dicotyledons 13, **35**, 53, 59
dioecious **29**, 59
dispersal **34**, 59
divisions (plant kingdom) **53**
dominant genes **54**, 59
dormant seed **35**

drupes **32**, 59
drupelets **32**, 59
dry fruit **33**, 59
duckweed **38**

E

early wood **15**
ecosystem **48**
embryos **32**, 59
emergent plants **38**, 59
endodermis **13**, 59
endosperm **30**, 59
entire leaf margin **17**
enzymes **25**, 43, **59**
ephemeral **59**
    plants **47**
epidermis **13**, 18, **59**
epigeal germination **35**, 59
epiphytes **24**, 59
eutrophication **39**, 59
evergreen trees **47**
exodermis **13**, 59

F

false fruit **32**, 59
farming **49**
ferns 16, 36, 40, **41**, 53
fertilization **30**, 59
fertilizers 39, **49**
fibres **12**, 59
fibrous roots **11**, 59
filaments **29**, 59
florigen **27**, 59
flower shapes **31**
flowering plants **28-31**, 32-39
flowerless plants **40-41**
fluid movement in plants **20-21**
foliage **16**
food **49**, 56
    production in plants 8-9, 16, 18-19, **22-25**
forests **48**
fronds 39, 41, **59**
fruit **32-35**
fruiting bodies **42**, 59
fungi 24, **42-43**, 51, 52, 59
funicles **29**, 59

G

gametes **28**, 59
gametophytes **41**, 59
garlic **36**, 56
gemmae **41**, 59
genes 49, **54-55**, 59
genetic engineering **55**, 59
genetic modification 49, **55**, 59
geotropism **26**, 59
germination **35**, 59
gills (fungi) **42**
ginkgoes **53**, 59
global warming **51**
glucose **59**
GM food **49**, 55, 59
gnetae **53**, 59
grain **33**
grasses 18, 44, 48, 52
greenhouse effect **51**
ground tissue **9**, 59

growing point (in a root) **11**
growth **10**, **14-15**
    season **46**
guard cells **18**, 59
guttation **21**, 59
gymnosperms **53**, 59

H

halophytes **44**, 59
haptotropism **27**, 59
haustoria **24**, 59
heartwood **15**
hemiparasites **24**, 59
herbaceous **59**
    perennials **46**
heredity **54**, 59
hermaphrodites **29**, 59
hilum **32**, 59
holdfasts **39**, 59
holly 29
horsetails 40, **53**, 59
host **24**
hydrophytes **38**, 59
hydrotropism **26**, 59
hyphae **42**, 59
hypogeal germination **35**, 59

I

incomplete dominance **59**
insects 30
intensive farming **49**
internal respiration **23**, 59
internodes **10**, 60

K

kernel **33**
key fruit **33**, 60
kingdoms **52**

L

laminae **16**, 60 (lamina)
late wood **15**
lateral
    buds **10**, 60
    roots **11**, 60
leaf
    margins **17**
    scars **19**, 58 (abscission layer)
    stalks **19**
    traces **19**, 60
leaflets **16**, 58 (compound leaf)
leaves 9, 12, **16-19**, 52
legumes **33**, 34, 50, 60
leguminous **60** (legume)
lenticels **15**, 60
lettuce 49
lichens 48, **51**, 60
lightning 50
lipped flowers **31**
lithophytes **45**, 60
liverworts 12, **40**, 53, 60
lobes (of a leaf) **17**, 52
long-night plants **27**

M

mangroves **11**

masking **54**, 60
medicine 56
meiosis **60**
meristems **10**, 60
mesophyll **18**, 60
micropropagation **37**, 60
micropyle **30**, 60
microscope 8
midrib (in a leaf) **18**, 60
mildews **42**, 60
mimosa 27
minerals 11, 18, 20, **60**
mistletoe 24
mitosis **9**, 60
monera **52**, 60
monocotyledons 13, **35**, 53, 60
monoecious **29**, 60
mosses **40**, 45, 53
moulds **42**, 60
mountains 48
mycelium **42**, 60
mycorrhizae **42**, 60

N

natural selection **44**, 60
nectar **28**, 60
  guide **30**
nectaries **28**, 60
needles (of conifers) **48**
negative tropism **26**, 60 (tropism)
night-neutral plants **27**
nitrates 49, **50**, 60
nitrogen **50**
  cycle 43, **50**, 60
nitrogen-fixing bacteria **50**, 60
nodes **10**, 60
non-vascular plants **53**
nucleus 8, 9, 12, 52, 60
nuts 33

O

opposite leaves **17**
organelles **8**, 60
organic farming **49**
ovaries **29**, 30, 60
ovules **29**, 30, 32, 60
oxygen 22, 23, 50

P

palisade
  cells 9, **18**, **22**, 60
  layer **18**, 60
palmate leaves **16**, 60
parasites **24**, 60
parenchyma **13**, 60
penicillin **43**, 56
perennials **46**, 60
perfoliate leaves **17**, 60
pesticides 49
petals **28**
petioles **19**, 60
phellogen **15**, 60
phloem **12**, 14, 60
photoperiods **27**
photoperiodism **27**, 60

photosynthesis 16, **22**, 23, 24, 35, 51, 52, 60
phototropism **26**, 60
pigments 19, 39
pinnae **16**, 60
pinnate leaves **16**, 60
pistils **29**, 60
pistillate flowers **29**, 60
pitcher plant **25**
plant
  cells **8-9**, 18
  food **22-25**
  lifestyles **46-47**
  sensitivity **26-27**
  tissue 9, **12-13**
plasmolysis **21**, 60
plum **32**
plumules **32**, 35, 60
pods **33**, 60
pollen **29**, 30-31, 60
  tubes **30**, 60 (pollination)
pollination 28, **30-31**, 33, 60
pollution 51
pomes **32**, 60
poppies **28**, 30, 44
positive tropism **26**, 61 (tropism)
potatoes 36
prairies 48
primary
  phloem **12**
  roots **11**, 60
  tissue (plant) **12**
  xylem **12**
prop roots **11**
protective adaptations **45**, 60
proteins 50, **60**
prothalli **41**, 60
protista **52**, 60
pure-breeding **55**

R

radicles **32**, 35, 60
Rafflesia plant **24**
receptacles **28**, 32, 60
recessive genes **54**, 60
reed mace 38
reproduction **28-37**, **40-41**, 60
respiration, internal **23**
rhizoids **40**, 61
rhizomes **36**, 41, 53, 61
rock plants **45**
root **11**, 13, 20
  cap **11**
  hairs **11**
  pressure **20**, 61
  vegetables **11**
rosettes **17**, 61
rosy periwinkle 56
runners **36**, 61

S

saline **44**, 60
salt
  bladders **44**
  marshes **44**
samara **33**, 61
saprotrophic plants **24**

saprotrophs (saprophytes) **24**, 43, 61
sapwood **15**
scrublands **48**
seaweeds 39
secondary
  buds **10**, 61
  phloem **14**
  roots **11**, 61
  thickening **14-15**, 61
  tissue **14**
  xylem **14**
seed leaves **35**, 61
seedlings **35**
seeds **32-35**, 53
selective breeding **49**, 55, 61
self-pollination **30**, 61
sepals **28**, 61
serrate **61**
  leaf margin **17**
sexual reproduction **28-31**, 61
shingle beaches 44
shoots **10**, 61
short-night plants **27**
side veins **18**
sieve
  plates **12**, 61
  tubes **12**, 61
simple leaves **16**
sori **41**, 61
specialization **61**
  in plant cells **9**, 28
spine (in a leaf) **17**, 44
spiral leaves **17**
spongy
  cells 9, **18**, 61
  layer **18**, 61
sporangia **40**, 61
spores **41**, 42, 53, 61
sporophytes **41**, 61
sporulation **41**, 61
spring wood **15**
stalk, leaf **19**
stamens **29**, 61
staminate flowers **29**, 61
starch **22**, 61
stems **10**
steppes **48**
stigmas **29**, 61
stimulus **26**
stipules **17**, 61
stolons **36**, 61
stomata **18**, 20, 61
strawberries **32**
strobili **40**, 61
styles **29**, 61
submergent plants **38**, 61
succulent fruit **32**, 61
summer wood **15**
sundews **25**
sunlight **18**, 22-23
survival **44-45**
sycamores 33
symbiotic relationship **43**, 61

T

tap roots **11**, 61
temperate **61**
  grasslands **48**
tendrils **17**, 61

terminal buds **10**, 61
ternate leaves **16**, 61
testa **32**, 61
thallus **40**, 61
thigmotropism **27**, 61
tissue **9**, **12-15**, 61
tracheids **12**, 61
traits **54**, 59 (heredity)
transgenic **55**, 61
translocation **20**, 61
transpiration **20**, 21, 50, 61
  stream **20**, 61
trees **14-15**, 46
trifoliate leaves **16**, 61
tripinnate leaves **16**, 61
tropical **61**
  grasslands **48**
  rainforests **48**
tropism **26**, 61
true fruit **32**, 61
tubers **36**, 61
tundra 48, 61
turgid **21**, 61
turgor **21**, 61

V

vacuoles 8, 21, 61
variegated leaves **19**, 61
vascular **61**
  bundles **13**, 14, 61
  cylinders **14**, 61
  plants **12-13**, 53
  tissue 9, **10**, **12-13**, 18, 20, 39, 40, 41, 53
vegetative
  propagation **36**, 61
  reproduction **36**, 61
veil (in fungi) **42**
veins **18**, 61
venation **18**
Venus flytraps **25**
vessels **12**, 15, 61

W

water 8-9, 10-11, 12-13, 17, 20-21
  cycle **50**
  plants **38-39**
whorls **17**, 61
wilting **21**, 61
wind pollination **31**
wood **14-15**
woody
  perennials **46**
  plants **14**, 61

X

xanthophylls **19**, 61
xerophytes **44**, 61
xylem **12**, 14, 20, 61

Y

yeast 42, **43**, 61

Z

zone of elongation **11**, 61
zygote **30**

ACKNOWLEDGEMENTS

PHOTO CREDITS
(t = top, m = middle, b = bottom, l = left, r = right)

Corbis: 8-9 (b) Science Pictures Limited; **9** (m) Lester V. Bergman; **10** Richard Hamilton Smith; **12-13** Richard Hamilton Smith; **15** (ml) Bill Varie; **16** (t) Paul A. Souders; **17** (b) Scott T. Smith; **18-19** (t) Paul A. Souders; **24** (l) Kevin Schafer; **25** (main) Bill Ross; **26-27** (b) Ron Watts; **28-29** (b) Ralph A. Clevenger; **29** (br) Lee Snider; **30** (t) Darrell Gulin; **31** (b) Philip Marazzi, Papilio; **32** (t) Marko Modic; **33** (b) Australian Picture Library; **34** (r) Kevin Schafer; **36** (bl) Marlen Raabe; **36-37** (t) Richard Hamilton Smith; **37** (bl) Ed Young; **41** (tr) Raymond Gehman; **42** (t) Sally Morgan, Ecoscene,(b) Buddy Mays; **43** (tr) Kevin R. Morris; **44-45** (main) Joseph Sohm/ChromoSohm Inc; **45** (l) Richard Cummins; **46-47** (t) W. Wayne Lockwood M.D; (b) Joseph Sohm/ChromoSohm Inc; **48-49** (main) Galen Rowell; **49** (l) Hulton-Deutsch Collection; **50-51** (b) Raymond Gehman.
© **Digital Vision**: 1, 2-3; 4-5; 6-7; 29 (tr); 44 (bl); 47 (m), (r); 52 (tr); 52-53; 55; 56.
Science Photo Library 38-39 (t) Jan Hinsch; **Telegraph Colour Library** 14-15 (main); 25 (tr); 40 (b); **Britstock-IFA** 20-21 (t), 26 (t) **Powerstock/Zefa** 34-35 (main)
Still Pictures 18 (bl) Klein/Hubert; **The Stock Market** 22, 38 (bl)
Undersea Research Programme (NURP) 39 (mr)
Tony Stone cover Bob Torrez

ILLUSTRATORS
Simone Abel, Sophie Allington, Jane Andrews, Rex Archer, Paul Bambrick, Jeremy Banks, Andrew Beckett, Joyce Bee, Stephen Bennett, Roland Berry, Gary Bines, Isabel Bowring, Trevor Boyer, John Brettoner, Gerry Browne, Peter Bull, Hilary Burn, Andy Burton, Terry Callcut, Kuo Kang Chen, Stephen Conlin, Sydney Cornfield, Dan Courtney, Steve Cross, Gordon Davies, Peter Dennis, Richard Draper, Brin Edwards, John Francis, Mark Franklin, Peter Geissler, Nick Gibbard, William Giles, Mick Gillah, David Goldston, Peter Goodwin, Jeremy Gower, Teri Gower, Terry Hadler, Alan Harris, Nick Hawken, Nicholas Hewetson, Christine Howes, John Hutchinson, Ian Jackson, Hans Jessen, Karen Johnson, Richard Johnson, Elaine Keenan, Aziz Khan, Stephen Kirk, Richard Lewington, Brian Lewis, Jason Lewis, Steve Lings, Rachel Lockwood, Kevin Lyles, Chris Lyon, Kevin Maddison, Janos Marffy, Andy Martin, Josephine Martin, Rob McCaig, Joseph McEwan, David McGrail, Malcolm McGregor, Dee McLean, Annabel Milne, Robert Morton, Paddy Mounter, Louise Nevet, Martin Newton, Louise Nixon, Steve Page, Justine Peek, Maurice Pledger, Mick Posen, Russell Punter, Barry Raynor, Mark Roberts, Michael Roffe, Michelle Ross, Simon Roulstone, Graham Round, Michael Saunders, John Scorey, John Shackell, Chris Shields, David Slinn, Graham Smith, Guy Smith, Peter Stebbing, Ian Stephen, Sue Stitt, Stuart Trotter, Robert Walster, Craig Warwick, Ross Watton, Phil Weare, Hans Wiborg-Jenssen, Sean Wilkinson, Gerald Wood, David Wright, Nigel Wright.

Every effort has been made to trace the copyright holders of the material in this book. If any rights have been omitted, the publishers offer to rectify this in any future edition, following notification.